Sunset Echoes

by
Rev. J.A. Wood

Author of
Autobiography of John Allen Wood
Mistakes Respecting Christian Holiness
Perfect Love
Purity and Maturity
Wesley on Perfection

Schmul Publishing Company
Nicholasville, Kentucky

COPYRIGHT © 2017 BY SCHMUL PUBLISHING CO.
All rights reserved. No part of this publication may be reproduced or used in any form or by any means — graphic, electronic, or mechanical, including photocopying, recording, taping, or information storage or retrieval systems — without prior written permission of the publishers.

Churches and other noncommercial interests may reproduce portions of this book without prior written permission of the publisher, provided such quotations are not offered for sale — or other compensation in any form — whether alone or as part of another publication, and provided that the text does not exceed 500 words or five percent of the entire book, whichever is less, and does not include material quoted from another publisher. When reproducing text from this book, the following credit line must be included: "From *Sunset Echoes* by J.A. Wood, © 2017 by Schmul Publishing Co., Nicholasville, Kentucky. Used by permission."

Cover image Copyright: <a href='https://www.123rf.com/profile_tntemerson'>tntemerson / 123RF Stock Photo</a>. Used by permission.

Published by Schmul Publishing Co.
PO Box 776
Nicholasville, KY 40340
USA

Printed in the United States of America

ISBN 10: 0-88019-606-8
ISBN 13: 978-0-88019-606-2

Visit us on the Internet at www.wesleyanbooks.com, or order direct from the publisher by calling 800-772-6657, or by writing to the above address.

Contents

	PREFACE	5
1	ENTIRE SANCTIFICATION	7
2	BACKSLIDING FROM ENTIRE SANCTIFICATION	11
3	DIVINE MANIFESTATIONS	15
4	ON TO HOLINESS OR BACK TO PERDITION	19
5	BLOW THE TRUMPET LONG AND LOUD	23
6	WHY DO SO MANY LOSE PERFECT LOVE?	27
7	FROM GLORY TO GLORY	31
8	THE PERSONALITY AND DIVINITY OF THE HOLY SPIRIT	35
9	DO ALL TO THE GLORY OF GOD	39
10	CHRISTIAN ASSURANCE	43
11	SCRIPTURAL ASKING	47
12	HOLINESS IN THE LIFE	51
13	PERFECTION	55
14	THE TURPITUDE OF SIN	59
15	SINS OF OMISSION	65
16	DEATH DOES NOT SANCTIFY THE SOUL	69
17	CONSCIENCE AND DUTY	73
18	A BAPTISM OF LOVE	75
19	THE REST OF FAITH	79
20	DIVINE VISITATIONS	83
21	WALKING ALONE WITH JESUS	87
22	THE CHRISTIAN PASTOR'S RESPONSIBILITIES	91
23	"HAVE ANY OF THE RULERS BELIEVED ON HIM?"	95

24	The Death of Saints	101
25	Ministers Need the Holy Spirit	103
26	The Vine with its Branches	107
27	The Bliss of the Purified	111
28	The Joy of Salvation	115
29	Regeneration with its Concomitants	119
30	Some Entirely Sanctified in all Denominations	123
31	Holiness is Religion Made Easy	125
32	Why God Delays Answer to Prayer	127
33	The Blessedness of Purity	131
34	How to Preach Well	135
35	The Self-Perpetuating Power of Sin	139
36	"The Sword of the Lord and of Gideon"	143
37	The Atonement	147
38	"Holiness to the Lord"	149
39	Sanctification Through the Truth	153
40	Charity and Humility	157
41	Reasons why More are not Entirely Sanctified	161
42	Needless Singularities	165
43	"Sinless Perfection"	169
44	Mistakes Regarding Entire Sanctification	173
45	Entire Sanctification Distinct from Justification and Regeneration	175
46	The Holiness and Happiness of All Men	179

Preface

In this little volume I present a series of articles written for various religious papers during years past; in this way giving them a more permanent form, and putting them where they may reach some who have never seen them. As it is not given to any man to know everything, I believe it wise for men to confine themselves largely to mastering the truths relating to their profession or life work.

My reading, thinking and writing during the past fifty years have been confined largely to evangelical truth, as related to the teaching and work of the Gospel minister. I make no claim to originality, and have no speculative, or novel notions; but have studiously sought to gather truth from every available source, and wherever I have found a clear, strong, important truth I have made it my own; and have thus filled my mind with Gospel truth, and incorporated it into my writings and preaching.

The reader may find some repetition in some of the articles, and may have seen some of them, or parts of them in various periodicals for which I have written. I trust the sentiments, principles and doctrines presented will be found helpful and useful. That they may do good and no harm is my prayer in giving them this book form.

—JOHN A. WOOD
South Pasadena, Calif., Dec. 14, 1904

1
ENTIRE SANCTIFICATION

I DO NOT INTEND, or assume to be an umpire on the subject of this article. I would write less on the subject, and give it less attention if others would write more, and give the doctrine and experience the attention its interest and prominence demand. It is the "central idea" of Christianity and as such is every way identified with the church of God and human salvation.

The word "sanctification" is quite common in both the Old and New Testament Scriptures. It, with its derivatives, occurs over one hundred times, and generally is expressive of Christian character. Very few words expressive of Christian experience occur as often in God's word; and being given by inspiration, it has divine sanction.

The doctrine of Christian sanctification is held as a cardinal truth by the whole church, both Protestant and Catholic. In some form it is associated with every leading creed in the Christian world. The church differs as to some particulars regarding it; these differences relate to its time, its extent, and somewhat to the conditions of the work.

All agree that entire sanctification must exclude all that is sinful or morally wrong. The church differs to some extent as to what is sinful; some holding that only sinful acts are sinful, while others claim that sinful states involve guilt.

The authorized views of the Methodist Episcopal Church are not extreme, but midway between high Calvinism on the one side, and low Zenzendiovianism [sic] on the other. Our ground is medium, or middle ground. Truth is almost invariably found between extremes; this is true not only theoretically, but practically and experimentally.

High Calvinism on this subject is taught in the Westminster Confession of Faith, which is the doctrinal basis of the Presbyterian Church. In it we are taught:— "This sanctification is throughout the whole man, yet imperfect in this life, there abide still some remnants of corruption in every part, whence ariseth a continual and irreconcilable war, the flesh lusting against the spirit and the spirit against the flesh."

The low Zinzendovian view is found in the writings of Count Zinzendorf, in "Holiness the Birthright of all God's children," as held and given by Dr. Crane, and by Prof. Fairchild, of Oberlin College. This view is presented by Dr. J. F. Crane in his article in McClintock & Strong's Biblical Cyclopedia, as follows: "In the renewal of the soul at conversion whereby man becomes a new creature, a new man, which after God is created in righteousness and true holiness, the inborn moral depravity is removed from the immortal nature, which so far as the work of cleansing is concerned, is in that moment fitted for heaven itself."

The Arminian, or Wesleyan doctrine occupies the happy medium between these extreme views; it is given in McClintock & Strong's, as follows: 1st "That man by nature is depraved, so that aside from grace, he is unfitted for all good, and prone to all evil."

2d. "That, through the grace of God, this moral depravity may be removed in this life and man may live freed from it."

3d. "That regeneration begins the process of cleansing; but except in some exempt cases possibly does not complete it, a degree of depravity still remaining in the regenerate."

4th. "That the process of cleansing is in some cases gradual, the remains of evil nature wearing away by degrees; in others instantaneous, the believer receiving the blessing of a clean heart a few days, or even hours, after his regeneration."

5th. "That this great gift is to be sought for specifically, and is to be obtained by a special act of faith directed towards this very object."

6th. "That this second attainment is attested by the Holy Spirit, which witnesses to the completion of the cleansing, as it did to the regeneration which began it."

7th, "That this gracious attainment, thus attested by the Holy Spirit, should be confessed on suitable occasions to the glory of God."

Here are no extreme views. The Methodist Episcopal church takes middle ground in every particular; as to its time, its nature, its conditions, and its limitations. As to its time, High Calvinism teaches that entire sanctification is never attained in this life. Low Zinzendovianism teaches that it is obtained at regeneration or conversion. The Methodist Church holds to neither of these extremes, but that between conversion and death we may be cleansed from all sinful proclivities and filled with love; that it is not commonly, if ever, received at conversion on the one hand, and need not be deferred until death on the other.

As to its nature, we hold it to be relative, hence limited by the capacity and capabilities of fallen human nature. It is not regarded as a superhuman, sublimated, angelic condition on the one hand, nor is it placed down on the level of sinful affinities or vicious appetites on the other. We teach the plain Bible presentation of devotion and purification, involving entire consecration of will, and entire cleansing of human nature—comprehensive essentials of *consecration* and *purity*.

We take medium ground as to its conditions. The work is partly divine and partly human. Submission, faith and co-operation with divine agency is human. Humiliation, conviction and assisting grace, and cleansing power are divine—God's work.

We avoid extreme views as to the guiltiness and nature of depravity. Some hold that there is damning guilt in depraved inclinations, while others hold that there is no moral guilt in depravity, and that guilt can be asserted only of sinful actions. The Methodist view is, that sinful acts alone involve guilt and need pardon, and that depraved states have moral quality, and hence need cleansing. We avoid confounding sinful acts and sinful states, that which needs pardon, with that which needs cleansing.

The agreements of the Christian Church on this subject, are however, more than their disagreements. All schools of theology agree, that the complete sanctification of believers is an essential part of the plan of salvation. All agree in pronouncing sin as a thing to be abhorred, repented of, and forgiven; and depravity a defilement of nature from which God's people must be delivered before they can enter heaven. All agree that the true followers of Christ hate sin, loathe it, resist it, turn away from it, and seek deliverance from it. All sensible Christians agree that no man can attain absolute perfection in any respect, at any time, or in any thing.

2
BACKSLIDING FROM ENTIRE SANCTIFICATION

NO STATE OF GRACE in this life excludes exposure from loss, or liability to backslide and apostatize. It is not uncommon for those entirely sanctified to lose ground and find themselves in part, or wholly backslidden. There is no necessity for this, and it certainly ought not to be.

Backsliding is a matter of degrees, whether from entire sanctification or from justification. It may be slight and partial in either case, or it may be entire—ruinous apostasy. Christ, after commending many things in some, said, "Nevertheless I have somewhat against thee." Of others, it is said they made shipwreck of faith and of a good conscience. Such is the relation of faith to salvation, that when the soul makes shipwreck of it, piety goes overboard with it.

Not every degree of backsliding forfeits either justification or entire sanctification. There may be some loss in either state without a forfeiture of all grace, or a gracious condition. There is, not infrequently, some little remissnesses, both in things omitted or committed, which tend to darken our light, weaken our strength, lessen our spiritual life, and render uncertain our assurance of divine favor; which do not plunge the soul at once into condemnation and death. These should be avoided as injurious and tending to utter apostasy. They are such as occasionally vain and useless thoughts, needless, idle words, little portions of misspent time, brief seasons of hesitancy in confessing Christ, slight remissions in prayer, or in reading the Bible, slackness at times, little self-indulgences, such as occasionally overeating or lying in bed longer than is needful or healthful, and over-indulgence in the lawful physical appetites, unnecessary lightness mixed with seeming irreverence and carelessness. I do not mean the habitual and worst form of these things; but as slight and occasional items. These, with many other like things, while they do not plunge the soul instantly into condemnation, do darken and weaken it, interrupt its communion with God, and gradually sink it into a doubtful and partially backslidden state.

In this way most of the backsliding occurs with those entirely sanctified; a remissness in little things, and a fall little by little. I call these items little things because they are relatively so in a comparative sense, and are along the line of things questionable and unquestionable. We are aware there is an important sense in which they are not little, and that with God nothing is either little of are not little, and that with God nothing is either little or great. "He that is unfaithful in that which is least, is also unfaithful in that which is much."

It is often asked, Can a believer backslide from a state of entire sanctification, and yet retain a justified state? That will depend upon how he backslides, and how far he backslides. When a man backslides by any voluntary known sin, properly so-called, he forfeits both entire sanctification and justification, and lays the foundation for repentance, confession and pardon, without which he will be damned just as any other unrepenting sinner. "He that committeth sin is of the devil," no matter what he possessed, professed or was before.

Every degree of backsliding, however, does not involve the loss of justification. A person walking in the light of purity, may, by almost imperceptible degrees, through various causes, lose his hold on Christ and the keeping spirit, and gradually lose the clear light of purity and still not forfeit his sonship as a child of God. Both pardon and purity are retained, as well as obtained, by faith, and we can maintain the light of purity only by the faith on which it is conditioned.

After justification and regeneration, when we were entirely sanctified, we received simply and only full spiritual cleansing; hence, the loss of what we received at that time would be the loss of purity only, and not of justification. As there are stages in the reception of salvation, it is reasonable to believe there may be stages in its loss.

"The just shall live by faith." "We stand by faith." "According to your faith be it unto you." There is a gradation in the scale of faith; there being "weak faith" and "strong faith," "little faith" and "great faith," and an "increase of faith." If there be an increase of faith, there may be also a decrease of faith, and a man may descend from "great faith" to "little faith" without a total loss of the principle of saving faith. We may backslide in a degree without backsliding totally, so as to be under the dominion of Satan. A believer may lose some ground without going over fully on to the devil's ground.

To suffer a decreasing light and a corresponding weakening evidence of God's favor, while under divine chastisement for little remissnesses, does not imply a forfeiture of heirship and all saving relations to Christ. A knowledge by the witnessing Spirit, of our acceptance with God, is not necessary in order to acceptance, of a state of either justification or sanctification. And yet, it is evident that the light of justification, after the loss of entire sanctification from any cause is less clear and assuring, and admits of more doubt and dissatisfaction; and usually restoration or apostasy is the alternative.

The difference between the regenerate and justified, and the entire sanctified, is in one possessing indwelling sin, and the other cleansed therefrom. It must be admitted that indwelling sin, a conscious sinful proclivity (sinful in nature and not in indulgence) does not involve the loss of justification, though it may lead to its loss. If this were so, all regenerated, but not entirely sanctified souls, could not be in a state of justification. This sinful inclination, whether felt or otherwise, is inconsistent with purity of heart.

Mr. Wesley taught that entire sanctification might be lost without the loss of all saving relation to Christ. He says, in speaking of backsliders from entire sanctification: "Sometimes suddenly, but oftener by slow degrees, they have yielded to temptation; and pride, or anger, or foolish desires have again sprung up in their hearts. Nay, sometimes they have utterly lost the life of God and sin hath reigned in dominion over them." Sermons, Vol. II, page 247. "The rest had suffered loss, more or less, and two or three were shorn of all their strength," Journal, 1763. "On a close examination (at Manchester) out of more than fifty persons, who two or three years ago were filled with the love of God, I did not find more than a third part, who had not suffered loss." Journal, 1766. "I returned to Chester, and found many alive to God, but scarce one that had retained his pure love." Journal, 1780. In these and in many other instances Mr. Wesley taught that the loss of entire sanctification does not necessarily include the loss of justification and all religious life.

3
DIVINE MANIFESTATIONS

THE WORD OF GOD TEACHES with clearness and positiveness that God will manifest Himself to the humble and devoted Christian. "He that hath My commandments, and keepeth them, he it is that loveth Me: and he that loveth Me shall be loved of My Father, and I will love him, and will manifest Myself to him." "If a man love Me, he will keep My words: and My Father will love him, and we will come unto him, and make our abode with him."

Here it is promised that God will manifest Himself in some special way to His children, as He does not to men in general. This manifestation to the soul refers more to illumination and spiritual apprehension than to faith. "We will come unto him, and make our abode with him," is a promise which has its fulfillment in our Saviour's declaration: "Blessed are the pure in heart: for they shall see God." They shall have such a clear spiritual apprehension of the existence and presence of God as serves as a practical vision, and it is as if they saw Him with open sight. This is more than mere faith; it is one of the blessed results of faith. It is experience, knowledge, and assurance.

This manifestation is by the Holy Spirit, and implies a visit or baptism of the Holy Spirit. Christ said: "If I go, I will send the Comforter, and He shall abide in you." The abiding Spirit of God in a fully sanctified soul makes the soul as much a knower of salvation as a believer in salvation.

> "Faith, Hope, and Love were questioned what they thought
> Of future glories, which religion taught;
> Now Faith believed it firmly to be true,
> And Hope expected so to find it, too,
> Love answered smiling with a conscious glow,
> Believe! Expect! I know it to be so."

This seeing and knowing is not physical, is not of the body, but of the mind. It is not by natural vision, not by physical senses, but by the internal eye of spiritual perception. Without running into fanaticism or vagaries, it may be said there is an important sense in which we may see God. Christ said: "The world shall not see me, but ye shall see Me." He did not mean that He would come again during their lifetime, and they should see Him, but that He would so manifest Himself unto them that they should know that He was with them, and that they had personal interviews and communion with Him. Where two or three are gathered in His name, His promise is, "There am I in the midst of them," and He closed His great commission to His apostles with the declaration: "Lo, I am with you alway, even unto the end of the world."

Millions of saints have had a manifestation of Christ to them, and many can now truthfully declare they have communion with Christ and they have seen the Lord. There is a moral standpoint of spiritual vision where Christ is apprehended as "the King in His beauty," as "the Rose of Sharon," as "the Lily of the valley," as "the Chief among ten thousand," as "the brightness of the Father's glory," and as "Emmanuel, God with us." It is not needful to wait until we reach the throne to have something of a gaze at the charming glories of the God-man. These manifestations of God break the charm of the world and lead the soul to exclaim:

> "Far from my heart be joys like these,
> Now I have seen the Lord."

These baptisms of spiritual light and vision are highly important to Christian ministers, enabling them to preach the Gospel with faith, love, and power. Men filled with the Holy Spirit, with their convictions intensified by the power of God, and minds illuminated with the spiritual manifestations of the presence and love of Christ, will declare, like John, "That which we have seen and heard declare we unto you." No man can preach the Gospel with efficient energy and in the demonstration of the Spirit without more or less manifestations of the divine presence. O what a joy to preach the blessed truth of God under the inspiring impressions made by these manifestations of the presence of Christ! It is a great calamity for a minister to lose the presence and power of Christ. All that such a man can say about the Gospel of Christ is cold and formal. He cannot preach as if he possessed, enjoyed, and knew the Lord. The Church needs a fuller baptism of experimental light and knowledge to lead a lost world to Christ. When God is sought with all the heart He will manifest Himself to His people in great power and glory. "Ye shall seek Me and find Me, when ye shall search for Me with all your heart."

4
ON TO HOLINESS OR BACK TO PERDITION

ALL PROGRESS TOWARD HOLINESS is on toward heaven, and all backsliding from holiness is back toward hell. In religious experience not to go forward, is to go backward. Strictly speaking there is no standing still in moral condition. It is either progression, or retrogression. Israel could not stand on the borders of Jordan, not to go over was to go back. The alternative after regeneration, is either entire sanctification or apostacy.

Thousands of Christian professors advance to certain points in Christian life, then pause, and then recede. Though indisposed to go forward, they fluctuate between life and death, and finally either consent to be holy and wholly the Lord's or entirely fall away. Whenever a believer is brought to see his need of perfect holiness, and his duty to seek it, and he refuses to yield fully to God and do his duty, he will inevitably go back, grieve the Holy Spirit, and drift toward perdition. All backsliding is in that direction.

What is the principal cause of so much backsliding among Christians? Why is the faith of so many weakened? their hope dimmed? their love cooled? their zeal abated? their meekness gone? their patience exhausted? their joy fled? their prospects blurred? their peace disturbed? and every other grace diminished? The plain truth is, they did not follow their convictions, yield fully to God and seek to be holy. Inbred sin was allowed to remain in their hearts, and as a result their peace, faith and love have been antagonized, stabbed, and choked by it. The remaining carnal propensities in the believer, foster pride, levity, anger, worldliness, self-indulgence and every other sin. Indwelling sin harbored will open the gates or avenues of the heart, for all kinds of unholiness to enter. The neglect of entire sanctification produces backsliding, while seeking, obtaining and retaining it, is an infallible remedy against it.

Young converts, generally are happy because for a time they are faithful to the light and grace they have, and they never need be any less happy than in the first stages of Christian life, but more, much more so, if they live up to their light and duty. Among the first lessons of the Bible and the Holy Spirit after conversion is to hasten on over into the Canaan of perfect love; but alas! how many when convicted of their indwelling sin and need of purity, refuse to go forward, content themselves with what they have experienced, and consequently start back and downward toward perdition. Unwilling to go forward, they take the back-track, and then come the dismal results of a wilderness state—discontent, perturbation of mind, painful doubts, gloomy fears, fiery trials and heavy crosses. The church of God is terribly suffering everywhere, with multitudes of backslidden professors, in just this unhappy, melancholy condition. Is it strange that the world thinks that religion must be a gloomy thing?

What is true of the members of the church, in this respect, is equally true of ministers who fail to press on after entire sanctification. If a minister neglects his duty, and fails to be a holy man, the work of grace in his heart will decline, his power and usefulness diminish, and he will become more and more a failure. He may study hard, and try to make up in earnestness, literary attainments, and hard work, but with a declining religious life and decreasing devotion to God, his ministry will be less and less satisfactory and useful.

When personal holiness is not sought, the natural results are more selfishness, more covetousness and self-indulgence, and less ardent, persistent successful work for God and souls.

When any Christian refuses to seek holiness he turns his back upon Christ, whose blood "cleanseth from all sin," and draws his heart away from fellowship with God. The result is barrenness of soul, fiery chastisements, and a scourge of many troubles. Those, who were once happy in God and happy in their work, now become subjects of distressing temptations, violent suggestions from Satan, and doubt that they were ever converted. God seems to suffer the devil to harass and distress them to drive them back to Christ. O, how many who were once full of peace, light, and usefulness have gone back, and have closed up their lives in doubt, shadows, and disappointments!

Backsliders, and apostates from Christianity are not only the most guilty, but the most unhappy of mortals. By refusing to go forward and seek holiness, they sin against greatest light, and become more miserable than ordinary sinners. The love of God withers and fades out of their hearts, and they become soured, jealous, dissatisfied, and seek relief in earthly pleasures, and become "worldly, sensual and devilish." "The latter end of them is worse than the beginning." They do not go on to holiness, but back to perdition. Reader, which way are you going? Are you headed, and making progress heavenward, or are you on the down grade? Which—on to holiness, or back to perdition?

5
Blow the Trumpet Long and Loud

THERE ARE BREAKERS AHEAD! The church of God is in the midst of increasing dangers! These are perilous times! Infidelity, the rum curse, and the devil and secretism more than ever are bold, active and rampant, while multitudes in the churches are either blind, asleep or dead.

There is a rising tide of unbelief, carelessness, recklessness, licentiousness, fraud, worldliness and ungodliness setting in around the church on all sides. How powerless many professing Christians, to resist these evil influences and exert good ones!

The way many churches are treating the duty and privilege of personal sanctification is manifestly displeasing God, and grieving his Holy Spirit.

The obligation to be pure in heart and entirely devoted to God, who can deny? Mark how God enjoins holiness, and how he enforces it, and how his appeals are rejected, and his provision for it neglected. He reveals his own unsullied holiness, and then commands his people to be holy as he is holy. He gives his own Son as an atoning sacrifice, whose precious blood cleanseth from all sin. He gives the church "exceeding great and precious promises," that she may be filled with the "divine nature." He furnishes us the Holy Spirit and commands us to "be filled with it," as a living, divine energy. He tells his church plainly that "Without holiness no man shall see the Lord."

How are these important and blessed truths treated by the mass of the church? Great multitudes doubt and deny the practicability of becoming holy as God requires, until death. The future life alone they set apart for entire sanctification; the present they regard as destined to mixed holiness and sin. That man can and ought to be saved from all sin in this life is regarded as rank heresy. Many of our fashionable churches will not endure the plain, faithful preaching of entire sanctification.

Unbelief is the great sin of these times, both within and without the church, and it is fruitful of the most alarming results. Nothing can be so fatal to the soul as unbelief. It always has been so. It is now so, and it always will be so, and I may add, it ought to be so. When the church harbors unbelief she forfeits her hold upon the promised strength of God, and like Samson, is shorn of her locks. Unbelief would paralyze the energies of an angel.

Oh! how much tolerating, countenancing and defending sin there is among church members. It gives place to the devil, displeases God and works ruin. This is that which we fear is gradually killing thousands of American churches which are cold and seemingly powerless to evangelize this world and bring lost men to God.

There never was a time, perhaps, when light and truth were poured in upon the church more than now, and the duty and privilege of being saved from sin and made pure in heart; and yet there probably was never half as much effort, learning, talent and philosophy expended to defend sin and hold on to it as now.

Christ came to put away sin; his blood cleanseth from all sin. He cannot and will not sanction any sin. When those who profess to be his people stand back from duty, and excuse, defend and hold on to sin, he will forsake them. This is the reason why the heavens over many of the churches are brass; they are pining and dying out, while infidelity, licentiousness, Sabbath desecration, drunkenness, rowdyism and the like are on the increase almost everywhere.

God has a controversy to-day with the Christian church for her unbelief, remissness, failure to put on her strength and come up to his help against the mighty. Millions are marching hellward, while the great body of the visible church are doubting, hesitating, or caviling over the duty and privilege of Christian sanctification.

It is as clear as the sun in mid-heavens that the pressing need of the church is holiness and power, evangelical, aggressive power. This is needed a thousand times more than anything else to save the church from her miserable wranglings, her cursing church trials, her paralyzing unbelief, her fairs, her festivals and church frolics, and from all torpidity, worldliness and spiritual death.

Satan is prowling around our churches, and backsliders are dropping out on every side, and this is no time for the ministers of God to sleep at their posts. The lines need to be more sharply drawn and the watchmen more bold, independent, and outspoken. Let Zion's watchman "cry aloud, spare not, lift up their voice like a trumpet and show God's people their transgression and the house of Jacob their sins."

> "Let Zion's watchmen all arise,
> And take the alarm they give,"

and let the trumpet be blown long and loud until millions come who are ready to perish.

6
WHY DO SO MANY LOSE PERFECT LOVE?

IT IS A SAD FACT that some, and perhaps many, lose the grace of perfect love, and some several times before they become established therein. The same fact is true, and much more frequent, in the loss of justification. It is a common thing for converts to lose the light and witness of justification many times before they become fully established therein. There is no necessity of this loss in either case, and we think there is much less danger of losing perfect love(other circumstances being equal) than justification.

The causes are very similar, and largely the same as those that cause the loss of justification. If the light of justification were more clear and general in the church, less converts would lose justification during their early experience; and, if the blessing of perfect love were more generally sought and possessed by the ministry, and membership, and more clearly and faithfully preached and exemplified in the pulpit, but few who obtain it would lose it.

It is to be feared that many lose the clear light and

experience of purity for the want of practical sympathy and wholesome instruction from the pulpit. People who possess full salvation, and are striving to love God with all their hearts, have a right to expect encouragement and help from the pulpit; but in many instances how little help they get from the defective and contradictory teaching given though there be no decided opposition to the subject.

Is it a marvel that some lose the witness and blessing of perfect love, if they be located where they find little or no sympathy for it, and where they do not hear more than a sermon or two a year on the subject, and those made up of indefinite generalities and cautions against high professions, such sermons as are frequently preached by those who do not possess the experience or are not earnestly seeking it?

Those possessing perfect love need help and encouragement from the pulpit, as well as those who do not possess it. The pulpit is the main place to present gospel truth, and feed all classes of Christian believers with the "bread of life." The plain fact is, the diluted, confused, crude and anti-evangelical notions, which many of our churches sit under, is anything but gospel preaching. It is a burning shame that many of our churches are pining and withering under pulpit administrations composed largely of short intellectual essays, scientific, metaphysical, geological, astronomical and speculative, full of almost everything except plain gospel truth. It is a serious question how long the Church of God can live on such pulpit matter. It is anything but the "bread of life," such as the Bible furnishes to feed, strengthen and establish the sons and daughters of the Lord Almighty.

Let sympathy in the Church become as general in favor of entire sanctification as it is for justification, and let it be preached with the clearness and frequency its importance demands, and let its possessors and witnesses in both the ministry and laity be treated as others are, and we shall hear of but few losing the grace. The condition of things in many of our churches is presented by Dr. Adam Clarke: "Most who call themselves Christians hate the doctrine of holiness; never hear it inculcated without pain; the principal part of their studies, and those of their pastors, is to find out with how little holiness they can rationally expect to enter into the kingdom of heaven." "Theology," p. 203.

Mr. Wesley rebuked some in his day the same way that some need in our day: "Those who love God with all their heart must expect much opposition from professors who have gone on for twenty years in an old beaten track and fancy they are wiser than all the world. These always oppose the work of sanctification most." He wrote to one of his ministers: "I hope Bro. C—— is not ashamed to preach full salvation receivable now by faith. This is the word which God will always bless and which the devil peculiarly hates; therefore, he is constantly stirring up both his own children and the weak children of God against it."

7
FROM GLORY TO GLORY

THE BREEZES OF PARADISE, sacred and divine, float about the word "glory;" it is inspired and identified with our interest and future blessedness. "But we all, with open face beholding as in a glass the glory of the Lord, are changed into the same image, from glory to glory, even as by the spirit of the Lord" (II Cor, iii:18). There are phases of religious truth, experience and divine manifestations to which this word "glory" refers.

It sometimes refers to the infinite perfections, grace and blessedness of God, at other times to the fullness, power and efficiency of the gospel; and not unfrequently refers to the experience, moral condition and blessedness of the Christian believer; on this last aspect I desire to write a few items.

The gifts of God in personal salvation are said to be "according to the riches of his glory." Our Savior said, "And the glory which thou gavest me, I have given them." Christians are exhorted to "walk worthy of God, who has called them unto his kingdom and glory." St. Paul says the Ephesian Christians were called by the gospel to the "obtaining of the glory of our Lord Jesus Christ." The Christians at Colosse were to be "strengthened with all power, according to the might of God's glory," and "possess the knowledge of the glory of God in the face of Jesus Christ." Paul says to Timothy: "The gospel of the glory of the blessed God was committed to his trust." The manifestation of God to his saints is "Christ in you the hope of glory."

This word in regard to the saints of God expresses a divine manifestation of extreme blessedness. God is pleased to permit the Christian to press into his manifest glory, and this glory of God is a personal experience in this world, and is preparatory to an "eternal weight" of divine glory in the heavenly world. This glory is to be actualized by the Christian, and begins and advances from stage to stage in this life, as is taught in II Cor. ii:18. "But we all, with open face beholding as in a glass the glory of the Lord, are changed into the same image from glory to glory, even as by the spirit of the Lord."

God has promised to be the glory in the midst of his people. Moses saw the glory and was so transformed by it that he covered his face with a veil, as the people could not bear the reflected light and glory. "For our light affliction, which is but for a moment, worketh for us a far more exceeding and eternal weight of glory." Dr. Adam Clark says, "This glory is a divine radiance so intense as to have weight—weight which is exceeding, and far more than exceeding—eternal."

This divine glory is susceptible of experimental demonstration in Christian experience. I will give a few witnesses. Many might be given. Rev. John Fletcher testifies to this experience. He says: "I was favored like Moses, with a supernatural discovery of the glory of God, in an ineffable converse with him, face to face: so that whether I was then in the body or out of the body, I cannot tell." Rev. William Bramwell says: "The glory I then experienced was beyond all I can now relate. I was filled with mercy and I could have shouted mercy continually."

William Carvosso, a prominent member of the Wesleyan connection in the days of Wesley, says: "I was one night in bed, so filled, so overpowered with the glory of God"... "Beholding as in a glass the glory of the Lord, I was changed into the same image from glory to glory by the spirit of the Lord." At another time he says: "Had he not veiled his glory in a moment, I could not have lived under it." President Charles G. Finney, for many years president of Oberlin College, and one of the most prominent evangelists of modern times, says: "As I came up to the door of the church, all at once the glory of the Lord shone upon and around about me, in a manner most marvelous... This light seemed to be like the brightness of the sun in every direction. It was too intense for the eyes... It was such a light as I could not have endured long."

Rev. Asa Mahan, D. D., LL. D., gives his experience as follows: "I now come to speak of a source of blessedness, to the description of which, I fear, I shall be able to make but a feeble approach. It is what, for want of better language to express, I would call those open, direct and inconceivably sweet visions which, a great portion of the time, I have of the infinite beauty, loveliness and ineffable glory of Jesus Christ and of the Godhead as manifest in him... It was a baptism in which the Son of Righteousness shone out in cloudless light, beauty, sweetness and glory, upon my soul."

Bishop L. L. Hamline wrote to his wife from the General Conference in 1844: "I often feel like a burning bush as I sit in the conference room. It is sometimes difficult for me to remain in my seat." At another time he writes: "Such blessings are poured upon me when I kneel in prayer that it seems as though I cannot live."

God has promised to manifest himself to his people as

he does not unto the world, and he has done it in all ages, and is doing it now to millions in the universal church. The repeated perusal of "The Real Christian," by Rev. S. P. Jacobs, a book of rare spiritual insight, has inspired this paper, and from that valuable book I have gathered and quoted some items in this article.

8
THE PERSONALITY AND DIVINITY OF THE HOLY SPIRIT

"But the Comforter, even the Holy Spirit, whom the Father will send in my name, he shall teach you all things," (John xiv:26). The proper personality of the Holy Spirit, as well as his divinity, is greatly ignored. The personal pronoun "it," shows the extent to which his proper personality is ignored.

Our dispensation—the Christian dispensation—is the dispensation of the Holy Spirit, and to ignore the personality of the Holy Spirit is a gross impropriety, whether done unwittingly or intentionally. "Where is your son John? It left home this morning, and it said it would be gone a month, and we miss it." If such usage would be derogatory to a man, how much more to the Holy Spirit? I am glad that the pronominal distinction of the Holy Spirit is always expressed in the Revised Version.

The personality of the Holy Spirit is the same as that of the Father and the Son, as seen in hundreds of passages and in all parts of the Bible. I give a few samples in which personality is seen. "The Holy Ghost said, Separate me,

Barnabas and Saul for the work," (Acts xxiii:2). "And while Peter thought on the vision, the Spirit said unto him, behold three men seek thee," (Acts x:19). "But the Comforter, which is the Holy Ghost, whom the Father will send in my name, he shall teach you all things," (John xiv:26). "He shall guide you into all truth. For he shall not speak of himself; but whatsoever he shall hear that shall he speak," (John xiv: 13).

The personality of the Spirit is taught in those texts ascribing to him volitions and affections; as "abide," "dwelleth," "teach," "testify," "searcheth," "grieved," "The Spirit also helpeth our infirmities... the Spirit himself maketh intercession for us." Manifestations of will, affections and works on the part of Christ taught his distinct personality, and they equally do the same regarding the personality of the Holy Spirit.

Personality manifests itself in thought, feeling and volition, and the Holy Spirit thinks, feels, wills and acts, and is therefore a Person. In our Articles of Religion it is clearly stated: "The Holy Ghost proceedeth from the Father and the Son, is one substance, majesty, and glory with the Father and Son, very and eternal God." The Holy Spirit is the object of trust, obedience and worship, equally with the Father and the Son. Baptism is in the name of the Father and of the Son, and of the Holy Ghost. All divine titles and attributes are ascribed equally to the three persons in the Godhead, and one is as much the object of adoration, love and devotion as the other.

The Father, Son and Holy Spirit, the Trinity in the divine essence, is such that the three Persons are externally equal in all essential being. In the plan of salvation the Father is supreme over the Son and Holy Spirit. This is only in official action, as has been well said, "All grace originates in the Father, is mediated through the Son and applied by the Holy Spirit." "For God so loved the world that he gave his only begotten Son, that whosoever believeth in him should not perish, but have everlasting life," (John iii:16). "He (the Holy Spirit) shall glorify me; for he shall take of mine and shall declare it unto you," (John xvi:14). See also John xiv:26.

Although the Holy Spirit is a Divine Person in the Trinity, according to the Scriptures and common usage, in describing things as they appear to us, it is appropriate to pray for the Holy Spirit to be poured upon us, as in our church ritual: "The Lord pour upon thee the Holy Ghost for the office and work of an elder in the church of God."

The Holy Spirit is the Executive of the Godhead, and is the divine agent, in conviction, regeneration and entire sanctification, and all the further work of illumination, intensification and growth in love, knowledge and holiness. The Holy Spirit reveals the Father and the Son to the soul of the believer: "No man can say (know) Jesus is Lord, but by the Holy Spirit," (I Cor. xii:3).

It is time that all Christians bear in mind in a practical way, and by an active faith in the divine personality of the Holy Spirit and not ignore him by calling him it, or a divine influence, or some other impersonal name. We may know the Holy Ghost; may be conscious of his sacred presence and enjoy blessed communion with him as the Third Person in the Holy Trinity. This is no fanaticism, but conscious religious experience, and in accord with Scripture truth. The Christian's heart is a temple of the Holy Ghost.

9
DO ALL TO THE GLORY OF GOD

THE INSPIRED DIRECTION is very plain— "Whether therefore ye eat or drink, or whatsoever ye do, do all to the glory of God." The glory of God is his praise and honor, and this is to be the great object of our pursuit. The term "whatsoever," in this passage, includes all our doings. All our acts, great and small, must have God's glory in view, for their end. His command takes in what are commonly considered small things— "Whether, therefore, ye eat or drink, or whatsoever ye do, do all to the glory of God."

This Scripture, like hundreds of others, covers the card-playing, theater-going and dancing question prominent at this time. If God is to be obeyed, our amusements and recreations should be regulated by this command. It is not advice; it is a divine command, plain and positive. If it is observed, the ultimate object in all our recreations must be "the glory of God."

There are times when relaxation is as much a duty as work, and a change in the trend of thought and pursuit is necessary to our health and usefulness. Not all pleasantry and merriment is wrong or injurious. Solomon says, "A merry heart doeth good like a medicine." But nothing should be indulged or done that either antagonizes Christ, or dissipates religious feelings. We should neither go anywhere, nor do anything upon which we cannot ask the blessing of God. Nothing should be approved, or indulged in inconsistent with the sacred, Christian profession.

The card table, the circus, the races, the dance hall and the theater are no places for Christian people. All of these are generally regarded by the Christian Church as injurious in dissipation and destructive of Christian character. They are more or less, sensuous, debasing and demoralizing, and are not in the "narrow way that leadeth unto life."

If rest, change and recreation be needed, there are plenty of ways which are consistent with righteousness and which do not compromise Christian character. Rest and change may be sought as wisely and piously as sleep. As to recreation, there are many innocent ways in which our languid spirits and exhausted strength may be reanimated and refreshed. The term recreation with many is about synonymous with dissipation, but its real meaning is to refresh, revive and reanimate. It is in this sense that the Christian can take lawful and needed recreation.

The foregoing Scripture furnishes us a rule for guidance in respect to all the customs and maxims of society. In so far as they can be followed to the glory of God, well; and when not, we should discard them, come out from them, be separate. Christians are to reform the world, and not be deformed by it.

Some people think those items are small things and of no special importance or consequence. This is a serious mistake. The sum of life is made up of little items, and the little items have more to do in the formation of our character and deciding our destiny, than the few great items, so-called.

An approving Christian conscience is impossible without observing the minutia of duty. There are, strictly speaking, no such things as small sins. They may appear so to dark and corrupt minds, but they are not so in the eye of God, nor in fact. All sin is a violation of God's law, and his law is one. The same authority enjoins every precept, and each sin involves a rejection of that authority. Every sin is rebellion against God, and that rebellion may be just as obstinate and offensive to God in small things (so-called) as in great things. It is never a small matter to disobey God. He or she, who frequents the theater, the dance hall, the races and the card table, does not live to the glory of God and should not be tolerated in the church of God.

10
CHRISTIAN ASSURANCE

Personal Christian testimony is an important part of all gospel preaching. St. Paul's commission reads as follows: "I have appeared unto thee for this purpose, to make thee a minister and a witness," Acts 26:16. The church has always conquered, as she has been a witnessing church to the "blood of the lamb" and by "the word of their testimony."

A witness is to testify to what he knows. Definite knowledge is the base of definite testimony. Personal testimony by the Christian is based upon the work and direct witness of the Holy Spirit. Only as one knows Christ and gospel truth by inward experience can he be an actual witness for Christ. "No man can say that Jesus is the Lord but by the Holy Ghost," I Cor. 12:3. The appointment of the Pentecost was to qualify the apostles by personal experience to be witnesses for Christ. "Ye shall receive power, after that the Holy Ghost is come upon you and ye shall be witnesses unto me both in Jerusalem and in all Judea," etc., Acts 1:8.

The direct testimony of the Holy Spirit is the safeguard

of Christianity. "The Spirit himself beareth witness with our spirit that we are the children of God," Rom. 8:16. "God who knoweth the hearts bare them witness, giving them the Holy Ghost," Acts 15:9. "Now if any man have not the spirit of Christ he is none of his," Rom. 8:9. "Now we have received, not the spirit of the world, but the spirit which is of God, that we may know the things that are freely given to us of God."

This direct and immediate witness or assurance given by the Holy Spirit, excludes doubt or uncertainty as to our pardon and acceptance from God. It unites together the divine and the human consciousness by faith in Christ. This assurance is the strongest possible that can be given of any fact in religion, science or nature. It is intuitive, and if anything is infallible, it is. It is not an inference, it is immediate self-consciousness, and the evidence of self-consciousness is infallible. John Stuart Mill says: "Whatever is known to us by consciousness is known beyond the possibility of doubt." John Wesley declares, "I judge it is impossible that this man (who has the witness of the Spirit) should be deceived therein, as that God should lie."

Luther, Melancthon and many of the reformers, frequently and strongly asserted that every believer is conscious of his own acceptance with God and that by a supernatural evidence. Sir William Hamilton, a Presbyterian, declares: "Assurance, personal assurance, was long and universally held in the Protestant communities to be the criterion and condition of true, saving faith."

Religious experience is experimental and positive. "The kingdom of God is within you," Luke 17:21; "The kingdom of God is righteousness, peace and joy in the Holy Ghost," Rom. 14:17. A knowledge of God and "the kingdom of God" is reported to our consciousness within the soul by the Holy Spirit. God is within the Christian and is as near him as he is to himself. Communion and fellowship with God implies this: "For ye are the temple of the living God, as God hath said, I will dwell in them and walk in them," II Cor. 6:16. The Father, Son and Spirit comes into fellowship and union with the Christian's spirit. This is not only a truth of revelation, but of consciousness and positive experience.

This blessed assurance is being largely neglected, ignored or rejected in the churches and multitudes of professed believers are living without the experience. Let it become general as it ought to be and it would resurrect our class-meetings and love feasts and give the church victorious power to bring lost men to Christ. Let the ministry of the church stand out clear in this experience and their notions of evolution and higher criticism will fade away like the mist of the morning. It will exclude all doubt as to the personality of God, or the divinity of Christ, or a supernatural religious experience by the Holy Spirit and the inspired word.

11
SCRIPTURAL ASKING

"WHAT THINGS SOEVER ye desire, when ye pray, believe that ye receive them, and ye shall have them." Mark 11:24.

There has been some difference of opinion in regard to the meaning of this passage.

This passage does not teach that any blessing can be received *independently* of the *established conditions* of its bestowment.

It does not teach that *faith* in the *fact* of receiving a blessing is the *condition* of receiving it. Such faith would involve the absurdity of believing it is *done*, and it *will be done*. The effort of faith is not to embrace the fact of receiving a blessing, so as to make the belief that we receive the condition on which we receive.

This passage does not teach that any are to believe they receive without a present, simple, appropriating faith in the merits of Christ.

It does not teach that any are to believe they receive without reasonable and proper cause for so doing. When a soul is dearly conscious of having complied with the terms of salvation, God's *promise and warrant* render safe and proper the belief that He now accepts and saves.

"Believe that ye receive them" — When? Just when you comply with the conditions; not *before* you comply with them, and not *after you have complied* with them. You are not to believe that you *receive* them after you have *got them*, on the one hand, or *before* you obtain them, on the other.

"And ye shall receive them." When? Not *before* you believe, but just *when* you *believe*, not *have* received, but that ye *receive just now* while you are *believing*. "According to your *faith* be it unto you," is the established order of God; and evangelical *believing and receiving* are inseparably joined together, and cannot be put asunder.

"Must I believe I receive the blessing just now, without evidence that I do receive it?" You are by no means to believe without evidence; but the evidences upon which your faith is to rest for the blessing now, are the promise, faithfulness, and certainty of God's word, and not your *feelings or imaginations*, which may deceive you. You are to *believe* that you *receive* on the authority of Jesus Christ, you, on your part, having complied with the divinely appointed conditions.

The *faith* that *saves*, that *claims* the promise, that *relies and walks out on God's word*, must precede the consciousness or interior witness of possession. There can be no room for *saving* faith after visible or tangible manifestations, or after the blessing is received. It is a matter of knowledge then.

Mr. Fletcher says: "Beware of looking for any peace or joy previous to your believing, and let this be uppermost in your mind."

You say: "I do not *see* and I do not *feel* any evidence that I receive the blessing." If you have *completely submitted* to God, you are to *believe*, and have no right to doubt God's word because of any absence of feeling. Your faith for salvation is not to rest upon *sight or feeling*. The

Bible says faith is evidence of things not seen. Faith in feeling, or in seeing, or in the witness of the Spirit, does not save; but faith, simple, naked faith in the word of God, does.

Seeing, feeling, and possessing the evidences of salvation must be subsequent to its reception. The blessing is conditioned on faith, and this faith must rest on the truth of God, as the evidences of possessing the blessing cannot exist before the blessing is received. Dr. True says: "I know of no way to obtain this salvation, but to follow the exact directions given: 'Believe that ye *receive*, and you shall have.'" Again he says: "You need not be afraid to *believe* that you *receive* while you pray; for, according to the testimony of thousands, you will thereupon *receive the direct witness of the Spirit*. This is what you have hoped to receive first, in order to believe; but it comes, if it comes at all, as the *confirmation* of your faith."

We can obtain salvation only by believing and trusting God. And an evangelical belief and trust in God can be exercised only in connection with complete submission to him.

Men are prone to live by *sense* rather than by *faith*, and are inclined to trust every thing and every body, but God. This passage teaches the great and important duty of *purely trusting and believing God*.

12
HOLINESS IN THE LIFE

A HOLY LIFE CAN emanate only from a holy heart, and a holy heart renders a holy life natural, easy and practicable. Purity of heart can be secured only by the cleansing blood and power of Christ; and it can be retained only by the pervading and keeping power of the Holy Spirit. The heart was made to flow through and pervade all our activities, and hence a holy life is the legitimate fruit or outcome of purity of heart.

A holy life includes abstinence from all wrong doing, and the doing all things pleasing to God. Its root principle is the spirit of obedience in entire consecration to God. A holy life involves several essential items:

1. It implies the seeking to know, as far as possible, the will of God; to study the Bible to learn His will, and to spend all necessary time in prayer for wisdom and guidance.

2. It implies that as far as possible, according to our best knowledge, we devote every power and faculty to the accomplishment of those objects which we believe God requires us to promote. Holy living requires

a supreme regard to the will of God in all things.

3. It carries with it, as far as possible, a right estimate of the relative importance of things— spiritual and physical, temporal and eternal; our own interests and other's interests; and that we give attention to things according to their perceived value. Holiness is harmony with truth and wisdom, and a life of holiness expands our powers, helps our infirmities, regulates our passions propensities and habits, and conforms in all things to the perceived will of God.

4. Living holiness includes not only supreme love to God, but equal and impartial love to our fellowmen. Our neighbor's interests must be regarded as of equal value with our own, so that we respect their rights as we do our own; their rights of property, their comfort, convenience, reputation and happiness, their improvement and salvation. With a holy man, if there be a failure in these respects, it is through mistake and not of design, and is only occasional and not habitual.

5. Holy living implies not only right activities, but right feelings toward God and man. A pure heart excludes all wrong feelings, and though our sensibility is not voluntary, yet when under the gracious power of the Holy Spirit we will possess such emotions of the sensibility as are proper in our relations to God and our fellows. There will be feelings of gratitude, love and complacency toward God, and feelings of sympathy, compassion, forbearance and brotherly love toward men.

All the emotions and feelings of a holy life are such as naturally exist in connection with the entire consecration of every faculty and energy to God. The pure heart carries the whole train of its affectional nature to God and humanity. One of the special works of the Holy Spirit is to bless, refresh and regulate the human sensibility. A holy man will not only act right but will feel right. Human feelings partake of moral quality, and as such are instruments of righteousness or of unrighteousness.

6. Holy living includes a conscience void of offense toward God and toward man. A constant aim to please God, with the best possible effort to do it, is all that God requires. The man who does all he can to please God, by the grace of God, is a holy man. We are obliged to do only what we can do, by the help of the Holy Spirit, and are not under obligation to do what we have no power to do. It is a self-evident truth that obligation can extend no further than ability. He who does all he has ability (both natural and gracious) to do, does all that God requires. It should not be forgotten that God will supplement human weakness by His most gracious ability, thus enabling all who seek His aid to do all His good pleasure. St. Paul says: "I can do all things through Christ which strengtheneth me."

13
Perfection

SANCTIFICATION, HOLINESS AND perfection are to some extent synonyms. They have shades of difference, but they are so slight as not to exclude their use as alternates to avoid tautology. Unsanctified humanity very generally possess a deep-seated prejudice against the term "perfection," when asserted of Christian character. When this term is used respecting anything but fully sanctified humanity, it is understood and generally approved. The inspired Word of God, which deals with things as they are and calls them by right names, uses perfection and its equivalents more frequently than any other term respecting Christian character and experience. The word perfection and its relatives occur one hundred and one times in the Scriptures. In over fifty of these instances it is asserted of human character under the operations of grace.

Perfection is simply completeness. It may be regarding things physical, intellectual, or moral. In the sense of completeness it is used almost universally, and no one objects to it. No one thinks of attaching absoluteness to it, nor do people find any difficulty in understanding it. Who ever heard it objected to, except in regard to God's saints?

Every created thing has its normal or necessary limits, while the uncreated God alone has absolute or unlimited perfection. There is a gradation which belongs to all the works of God, and there must be various sorts and degrees of perfection appropriate to each realm of being. Every creature of God may be perfect after its kind, and according to its nature and degree, and this term is just as legitimate respecting the lower grades as the higher.

We say a plant or tree is perfect when it has neither deficiency nor redundancy; having no defect in root, stem, leaf or flower. It possesses all that belongs to its sphere as a tree or plant. It may be smaller or larger, younger or older than some other tree or plant. It is complete in the sense of possessing all that is essential to it, or that belongs to it.

Angels are perfect according to their nature and capacity. They are perfect as angels, but are imperfect as compared with the absolute perfection of God. Christian perfection is graded according to the sphere and capacity of a man. When a Christian is complete according to his sphere of being and the dispensation in which he lives, he is a perfect Christian.

Let it be remembered God measures responsibility according to what a man hath, and not according to what he hath not. When this term is applied to Christians, as in all other cases, it is to be understood to mean a relative and modified perfection, according to the capacity, possibilities and facts of each individual case. Where much is given much is required. There is perfection in things small as well as in things great.

Fallen man, regenerated and fully sanctified, has his sphere in the mediatorial economy; and whatever that is is his perfection, and is Christian perfection. This in every case is a fullness of love, pure love in a purified soul. It is easy to see that this much abused term, when used respecting sanctified believers, is to be viewed in a restricted sense, and modified by the object to which it refers, the same as in other cases. In the nature of things the term implies limitations, except when applied to the unlimited God.

We notice that those who reject the use of this term, in respect to Christian character, affix to the word but one single idea, and that of *absoluteness,* implying absolute perfection. The error of applying absolute perfection to this Bible word, is very common with the opponents of Christian Perfection.

The Holy Ghost has employed this word, and it does not indicate humility to question the wisdom of its use. It is pushed into the foreground in Bible terminology, and it is folly to either reject the term or the blessed experience and life it expresses. Our Lord Jesus is a perfect and almighty Savior, and he can make his children perfect Christians. He can "save to the uttermost," and it is our duty and privilege to be saved from all sin and all sinfulness; from all *guilt* by a full pardon; from the *dominion of sin* by the power of the Holy Ghost; from all the *pollution* and the disposition to sin by the cleansing blood of Christ. It is herein that our love is made perfect, and we are enabled to love God with all our hearts and our neighbors as ourselves. Let as many as are perfect be thus minded.

14
THE TURPITUDE OF SIN

MUCH OF MODERN PREACHING is remiss in not presenting more of the nature, the turpitude and results of sin, and the necessity of salvation from it. Salvation is freedom from sin and its consequences. Jesus Christ came into the world to save sinners, and sinners are saved, only as they are saved from sin.

I have not written in respect to original sin; the corruption or infection of human nature—result of actual sin, but of sin as acts of disobedience.

Nearly all systems of unbelief minify sin, and regard it as a trivial matter and treat it accordingly. Men are usually governed by their views of things, and act in harmony with their opinion. "As a man thinketh so is he."

Sin, every sin, properly speaking is a violation or transgression of the law of God, by either commission or omission. This law is His written or unwritten will, a transcript of His mind, and the standard of moral rectitude in the universe. As such, it is perfect, impartial, just, necessary and divine. The law is holy and the commandment holy, just and good, and was ordained unto life. This law is the determination of all the moral attributes of God's nature, it emanates from the fountain of infinite wisdom, goodness, holiness and justice. Sin violates the demands of all these, and must be unwise, unholy and unjust.

It is an act of rebellion against God as the Ruler and Father of the human race; an act of the will of the creature, against the Creator. As such, it is against infinite wisdom, infinite justice, holiness and goodness. God says: "All souls are mine," and His right to govern all he creates and preserves is absolute. Sin despises the power and authority which forbids it. God is almighty, and He is our Law-giver and Judge. He is such by inherent right, and not by delegated right or power. He forbids sin and every act of sin despises the Almighty power which forbids it. The sinner refuses to respect the authority of God and His rightful claim as Law-giver and Judge. He practically challenges God to exert His power, and has no more respect for God's power, than if He had none.

Sin not only rejects divine authority, but it brings a curse and works ruin, not only to the sinner himself, but to all affected by it. While "the law was ordained unto life," sin changes that which tends to life, so that it is made death to the sinner. Violated law kills. Sin is such a ruinous, deadly evil, it turns the ministries of life into death. "The soul that sinneth, it shall die." "The wages of sin is death." "And sin when it is finished bringeth forth death." Life and death stand opposed to each other. The spiritual death of the soul signifies all the effects of sin, and includes the displeasure and curse of God; while spiritual life involves all the happiness and well being of existence, with the favor and blessing of God.

The vileness and detestable character of sin is seen in that it is an act of the basest ingratitude. Ingratitude is an odious and unnatural trait of character and many break friendship for life by it. The greater the goodness bestowed and the favors received, the baser the ingratitude. God is our Creator, our Father, our Preserver and Redeemer, and His bounties cannot be numbered. They exceed our comprehension. Looking upon ungrateful mankind, God exclaims in amazement: "Hear, O heavens, and give ear, O earth;... I have nourished and brought up children, and they have rebelled against me. The ox knoweth his owner and the ass his master's crib... but my people do not consider." "A son honoreth his father, but if I be a Father where is mine honor?"

God infinitely abhors sin, it is "that abominable thing," which His soul hates; and which is the most hateful, offensive, and ruinous thing in the world. The sinner stabs the hand that created, sustains and blesses him, and evinces an ingratitude as black as hell.

Sin is a practical rejection of God's mercy. Mercy is a disposition to pardon crime, and the sinner under the guilt of violated law, must have mercy or perish. While he is condemned and exposed to the curse of God, through the atonement mercy is provided and offered; but sin rejects and insults the God of mercy and crucifies the Son of God afresh. This is done while without the mercy, which sin rejects, he must perish forever. It is in view of this aspect of sin that our Lord asks: "How can ye being evil, escape the damnation of hell?" Sin is moral suicide. "He that sinneth against God wrongeth his own soul."

Sin involves enormous guilt as a violation of obligation. The guilt or turpitude of an action is equal to the amount of obligation violated. Our obligations to God may be estimated in several ways. They must be equal to our dependence upon Him; but our dependence upon Him is absolute and entire, and always has been, is now, and eternally will be. "In Him we live, and move and have our being." "By Him all things exist," and as John Wesley says, "Without his preserving power and hand all things would sink into its primitive nothing." His claims upon our obedience, must be equal to this dependence.

Again, our obligations to God, are equal to the blessings we receive from Him. God is a fountain of infinite benevolence to the universe and is the source and author of all blessings. His beneficence is infinite, and the blessings bestowed upon us are beyond our computation or comprehension. They include all the good we ever have had, or now have, or ever will have. What then must be the extent of our obligations to the infinite Giver of all blessings?

The demerit of sin is in proportion to the dignity and character of God insulted by sin. "How much sorer punishment, suppose ye, shall he be thought worthy, who hath trodden under foot the Son of God, and hath done despite to the spirit of grace."

The inherent malignity of sin is seen in this treatment of God, who is blasphemed, slandered, and insulted by the profane and atheistic of all classes. It denies His existence, it reviles His character, it spurns His authority and disobeys His laws. If we were treated as God is treated we could not find words to express our abhorrence and detestation of such conduct

The enormity of sin and the exceeding sinfulness of sin is seen in its self-perpetuating power—it is infectious, increasing in nature, and paralyzing in power all virtuous principles. It fixes habits of vice and makes wrong doing easy and natural, and renders a perpetual course of wickedness more and more certain. It quickens the susceptibility to temptation, it tends to overthrow all government and bring the authority of God into contempt. All sin, which is lawlessness, tends to universal lawlessness. In a word, sin tends to universal damnation.

The evil and wickedness of sin appear also in the manner in which God regards and treats it. If we turn to His word, we read: "O, do not this abominable thing which I hate." "The way of the wicked is an abomination to the Lord." The whole Bible is against sin, and its grand object is to lead men to avoid it and save them from it.

Look at His threatenings: "The wrath of God is revealed from heaven against all ungodliness and unrighteousness of men." "The Lord is angry with the wicked every day." "The wicked shall be turned into hell with all the nations which forget God." "Tribulation and anguish, indignation and wrath upon every soul of man that doeth evil." If sin is a trifle and not a deadly, fearful wrong, why does God thus threaten the sinner?

The way He regards sin is seen in His works and in His treatment of sinners. The whole history of divine providence is a war against sin. He spared not the angels that sinned. He drove Adam and Eve out of Eden because they sinned, and their sin has changed the whole current of human nature for six thousand years, and corrupted the whole race. Because of sin, as the whole race had corrupted its way, God destroyed the world with a flood. He sent fire from heaven and burned the cities of the plain because of their sins. He opened the ground and swallowed up thousands of His chosen people because they sinned. He has put the seal of His displeasure upon all the leading sins of wicked men, and hates sin now as much as He ever did.

It should not be forgotten that He is as much displeased with lying now as when He killed Ananias and Sapphira for lying. He is as much offended with Sabbath breaking as when He ordered men stoned to death for Sabbath desecration. He is as angry to-day with murder as when He put the mark on Cain and sent him out a vagabond in all the earth. He is as much opposed to covetousness as He was when He opened the ground and swallowed up Achan and his whole family. Licentiousness is just as offensive to Him as it was when He burnt Sodom. Disobedience was no more sinful when God killed Lot's wife than it is now. Unbelief is as ruinous as it was when Christ said: "He that believeth not shall be damned," or when the ten unbelieving spies were struck dead for their unbelief.

The same is true of pride—which is as hateful to God as when He smote Herod because of his pride. Well may the apostle declare: "It is a fearful thing to fall into the hands of the living God." Why all this, if sin is not exceeding sinful, and the foe of God and of man? It is the cause of all the evil in our world. It has ruined and degraded humanity, and what remains of our race that is praiseworthy are only the broken pillars of a once beautiful fabric. The corrupting power of sin has made man's desires sensual, his will perverse, his understanding dark, his conscience seared, his memory treacherous, and so alienated his affections that he is estranged from God, and his nature is degraded and fallen.

All our diseases and ailments and sufferings are the results of sin, actual or original, direct or indirect. This is true physically, intellectually and morally. It is inseparably connected with, and is the essence of all treachery, deception, cruelty, fear, fraud, oppression, murder and death. It has made our world a vale of tears and a field of blood.

We see why sin justly exposes to the wrath of God, as each sin combines all this violation of law, rejection of mercy, contempt of power, violation of obligations, base ingratitude and human degradation and ruin. It offers the greatest insult that can be made to the majesty of the great and glorious God, and is evil and only evil, root and branch, bud, blossom and fruit, a ruinous and abominable thing which has kindled a fire in God's "anger which shall burn forever."

15
SINS OF OMISSION

THEOLOGICAL WRITERS USUALLY CLASSIFY sins into those of commission and those of omission; meaning, by the former, overt acts of transgression, or the *doing* what should not be done; and by the latter, not doing what we ought to do, and not being what we ought to be.

This distinction stands related to a corresponding distinction in the moral law; since this both enjoins and forbids—requires some things to be done, and forbids the doing of certain other things. Neglect to obey its requisitions is a sin of omission; doing what it prohibits is a sin of commission.

Each of these classes of sin includes an internal state of mind, even when it results in no corresponding conduct, as well as our external doings or failures to do. Indeed, the only real sin is in the mind; and it may be manifested externally in natural development, or it may not be. In the latter case, it is none the less sin.

Most, if not all men commit more sins of omission than of commission; and in many cases the sins of omission are the more aggravated. There cannot be a more grievous sin, than not loving God; and there cannot be one more certainly, terribly and justly *damning than not accepting Christ as a Savior.*

In Matt. xxv., Christ represents the wicked at the final judgment as doomed to hell because they had not ministered to him in the person of the hungry, the thirsty, the stranger, the naked, the sick and the imprisoned.

It was not what they had done, that made and evinced their character, but what they had not done. They had not shown love to him, nor to his suffering friends. They evinced that they neither loved God nor man. Hence their righteous doom among the enemies of all good.

What a lesson the Savior here presents by this heart-searching representation! Oh! let us each examine, and see how our account stands of things not done,—the hungry not fed, the naked not clothed, the sick not visited, and the poor and needy not ministered unto.

There is a vast amount of self-deception among sinners and many professed Christians, the result, in a great measure, of not considering this aspect of sin.

Multitudes, all about us, have no just sense of their own moral turpitude. Why? Because they make no account of sins of omission. They do not look at the law of God, requiring them to love God supremely, and their fellowmen as themselves; and hence they see not their chief guilt. As to sins of commission, they find themselves by no means among the most scandalous sinners of the race. Hence, the ruinous estimate of themselves, which deludes their guilty souls.

Then, what a dense throng of merely nominal Christians, whose outward Christianity is at least so fair as to subject them to no church discipline or censure; but oh! the things not done,—the fervent prayers not offered; the crosses not borne; the self-denial and sacrifice for Christ not made; the daily efforts to save souls not put forth; the thousand nameless testimonies of love to Christ, which burst forth at countless points where that love really burns within, which are not given.

How will these deeds and duties not done rise up at last and testify against these professors in that day, when God shall judge the world in righteousness, by Jesus Christ, and put an end to every hope that is not eternal!

The precious doctrine of entire sanctification by no means overlooks sins of omission. On the contrary, it seeks to set the heart right, and bring it into the permanent attitude of loving God supremely and our fellow-beings impartially.

Perfect love, as required in the Bible, is that very state in which the inner spirit worships God, and loves its neighbor as itself.

16
DEATH DOES NOT SANCTIFY THE SOUL

PRACTICALLY, MULTITUDES IN THE church say they expect to be sanctified by the death of the body. They may not proclaim it in words, but their actions speak plainly. The greater part of professed Christians defer their full sanctification until death, while death itself has no more to do with their sanctification than with their pardon or justification. This mistaken idea is fruitful of nothing but evil, and millions are being deluded by it. All through the church are multitudes who are not entirely sanctified, and are looking forward to death for the completion of the work and their fitness for heaven. They are neglecting present duty and privilege, and presuming on a ruinous fallacy. The Bible nowhere states or even intimates that death sanctified the soul. It nowhere encourages Christians to look to death, or to rely upon it, for a completion of the gracious work commenced in their heart at regeneration. Where do we find the least intimation that Christ and the Apostles placed any reliance upon death for

Christian sanctification? I repeat, where?

While the sacred writers speak often of the means, the agencies, and the time of sanctification, they never name death as either its means, its agent or its time. Will those who are deferring their complete sanctification until death note this most ominous fact? If death sanctifies the soul, or finishes the work of sanctification already begun, then it, at least, is partially our savior; and the effect of sin (for "death is by sin") becomes the means of finally destroying it—that is, the effect of a cause can react upon its cause and destroy it. This would be a philosophical absurdity.

Death, in its very nature and circumstances, is entirely unpropitious for the work of sanctification. If, as the Bible teaches, sanctification involves human agency, the free intelligent action of the mind, "sanctified by faith," "through the truth," death is no time for such a process in cleansing the soul. Weakness and distraction of mind are the ordinary accompaniments of physical dissolution, and unfit it for calm and intelligent action. If death sanctifies the soul then the work is removed from the ground of moral agency, and the Christian has no responsibility in the matter. This would nullify all the precepts requiring human agency in obtaining personal holiness. That we have a personal responsibility in securing our entire sanctification, is as clear as that we have responsibility in our justification or partial sanctification.

In so far as we can see, there is not a shadow of evidence that dissolving the connection between the soul and body will produce any effect upon the character, or moral condition of the soul. The change produced by death is in our physical state and mode of being, and a mere physical change of state, cannot relieve the soul of its depravity, which is developed in its pride, unbelief, selfishness, corrupt lusts and sinward inclination. Sanctification is change of character, and change of character involves human agency, and is God's work, is by grace, through faith and moral means.

Many appear to hold the old pagan dogma that the body is the seat of sin, and that depravity pertains only to the body, and when the body dies, as the soul leaves the body it will be free from depravity. That the body has suffered by the fall and is degenerated and possessed of deranged appetites and propensities, making it an "instrument of unrighteousness," is admitted; but Christian sanctification has less regard to the body than the soul, which is the seat of inbred sin. The carnal mind, anger, covetousness, impatience, hatred and all filthiness of the spirit, belong to the soul and not to the body. The death of the body makes no moral change in the soul.

"In the place where the tree falleth, there it shall be," for "He that is unjust, let him be unjust still; and he that is filthy, let him be filthy still; and he that is righteous, let him be righteous still; and he that is holy, let him be holy still."

17
CONSCIENCE AND DUTY

It is not wise to always make our feelings a guide in deciding our duty. Impressions are made upon our minds by various agencies and objects, and they are not always safe to follow. In many instances they have led to great blunders, and sometimes to rank fanaticism.

"I felt it my duty to do thus and thus," has been often presented as an excuse for doing what has not been in harmony with either enlightened reason or the Word of God. When our feelings prompt us to do what is unsustained by reason, or the law of love and the Word of God, they should not be followed. The more nearly the soul presses to Christ, and seeks divine light and guidance, the more clearly the law of love and the Word of God will shine upon the mind, and the less likely the soul to go astray.

There are several rules of action which we think are always safe. When our convictions of duty are strong and clear, and are in harmony with our best judgment, the Word of God, and the law of love, we should always follow them. To follow such convictions, though they may not involve perfect wisdom, is right and safe. Humanity is not required to have perfect wisdom, but is required to do its best, to know its duty, and possess right convictions, and then be governed by them.

A mere impulse of feeling that a given course is duty, is not itself a rule to guide us, and should be sifted and tried by the Word of God and our enlightened judgment. God has given us the Bible, the illuminating Spirit, and our reason to guide us in the path of duty. He does not require us to do unreasonable things that contravene our judgment. The illumination and guidance of the Holy Spirit is always in harmony with the dictates of a godly judgment, with what is *right* and *wise* and *best* and *duty*, in view of all known facts and circumstances, and what is in harmony with the Bible. Reason is given us to exercise, in the light of the Bible and the Holy Spirit, in deciding our duty.

Impulses sometimes are from Satan. In this world we are subject to more or less Satanic influence. Dr. Payson tells us he sometimes felt a strong impulse to do, and do, and do, which was opposed to his cool judgment; and which, in yielding to, nearly killed him by overdoing, as he at first took the impulse to be from God. At last he concluded it was not like God to overwork His servants, and very like the devil to kill them by overwork.

18
A Baptism of Love

Love to God and to man is the dominating idea of the Christian religion. It is the controlling power in all true piety, and without it the Christian profession is as "sounding brass and a tinkling cymbal." Love is the inspiration and ruling influence in all acceptable devotion. While salvation is many-sided, this is the "central idea" and the principal thing. There is submission, adoration, illumination, regeneration, adoption, faith and hope; but love has the pre-eminence. "Above all these things put on love, which is the bond of perfectness."

In personal salvation nothing can be a substitute for love, as it is the distinguishing feature of the Christian life. "Love is the fulfilling (the substance and fulfillment) of the law." It is the root principle of all evangelical obedience; and he who loves God with all his heart will obey Him with all his power.

Love to God and evangelical obedience are inseparable. This is stated in a variety of ways: "And this is love, that we walk after His commandments." "For this is the love of God, that we keep His commandments." "He that hath My commandments, and keepeth them, he it is that loveth Me." "Whoso keepeth His words, in him verily is the love of God perfected."

"Pure love reigning alone in the heart," Mr. Wesley said, "is the whole of Christian perfection." "Now the end of the commandment is charity (love) out of a pure heart."

This love is the godly disposition of the pious heart. The realm of its operation is the whole soul, mind, and heart, subordinating everything to itself. It abides with the Christian, and becomes interwoven with his whole life. It is not an occasional impulse, but is to abide and pervade all his activities. Possessed in its fullness, it is a soul-filling, soul-controlling, and life-directing power—the supreme element in the life and conduct. Entire sanctification involves the fullness of this love, a disposition and abiding state of complete devotion to God.

This love is begotten or imparted by the Holy Spirit, and hence is received by a baptism. "The love of God is shed abroad in our hearts by the Holy Spirit which is given unto us." The blessed Holy Ghost is the efficient agent in the whole work of personal salvation, whether it be conviction, illumination, regeneration, or purification. After the work of salvation has been wrought, and after the heart is fully cleansed from all pollution, the influences of the Holy Spirit are needed to keep the living flame of love burning in our hearts.

This baptism of the Spirit of Christ and of love is usually preceded by self-abasement, spiritual poverty, and a distressing sense of spiritual deficiency. When the soul is humbled before God, emptied of self, and hungers and thirsts after righteousness, it will be filled with love to God and humanity.

How this is needed in these days of trial, danger, and responsibility! How it would relieve all disturbing collisions, nervous irritability, and sectarian distrust in the

Church! It is like Christ and heaven to have the soul full of love. O, when shall a full baptism of Christian love pervade the whole Church? What mighty revivals would break out in our places of worship! How sectarian antipathies would melt away! Such a baptism would blend all who truly love the Savior into the most tender Christian sympathy, and difficulties between brethren would be happily adjusted.

O, for a general baptism of love, to fill with peace and bless the Church of God!

19
THE REST OF FAITH

"For we which have believed do enter into rest." Heb. 4:3.

WE READ IN THE Scriptures, "A rest remaineth for the people of God." Christ said, "I will give you rest," and "ye shall find rest unto your souls." "The work of righteousness (says the Prophet) shall be peace, and the effect of righteousness, quietness and assurance forever." This soul-rest of a believer commences here, and now, and will be consummated in eternity. *Sin is a disturbing element.* "There is no peace saith my God to the wicked." Unregenerate humanity is like "the troubled sea." Our Lord came into the world as the *"Prince of Peace."* He was heralded with the joyous acclaim, "Peace on earth and good will to men." "Being justified by faith, we have peace with God." "Peace in believing." "My peace I give unto you." We inquire:—

I. WHAT IS THIS SOUL REST?

1. It is not a state in which we do not sympathize with

the joys and sorrows of others. The more fully saved and perfect the soul-rest, the more intense and active are all legitimate sympathies of the soul.

2. It is not a state of exemption from physical, or mental suffering— "The servant is not above his Lord." This rest is, however, a source of comfort and alleviation in the sufferings of life.

3. It is not a rest of inaction, or a state of inglorious ease. It is not stagnation or death, but life. Life and action are inseparable. The earth rests on its orbit, and yet moves with inconceivable velocity—out of its orbit it would be *disordered, restless and ruined.*

4. This soul-rest, in the justified and regenerate, is a state of freedom from the *reigning power of sin*. The minimum of salvation is salvation from sinning. "We know that whosoever is born of God sinneth not." "Whosoever is born of God, doth not commit sin; for his seed remaineth in him, and he cannot sin because he is born of God." "For sin shall not have dominion over you." "Whosoever abideth in Him sinneth not." These Scriptures teach that to be born again and savingly united to Christ, is incompatible with present actual sinning. All truly regenerate people have no disposition to sin; their controlling disposition has been changed, and they are inclined and disposed to love and obey God. Some of the rudiments of the old carnal disposition may remain in those not entirely sanctified, but the power of sin has been so broken, that the predominant disposition of the soul has been changed, and Christ's spirit rules in the heart.

5. In those fully saved it is a state of rest from all the jarring discords of indwelling sin. The disturbing elements having been removed, all internal conflict ceases. The soul has peace *with* itself and *in* itself. "The peace of God rules in the heart.

6. This rest is a state of sanctified adjustment of all the powers and affections of the soul. There is divine order

and internal harmony. All conflict between the will and the conscience and affections has ceased. "The peace of God, which passeth all understanding" (or as Dean Alford has it "surpasseth all understanding"), "shall keep your hearts and minds through Christ Jesus." It is a pure tranquillity [sic] of spirit.

7. It is a gracious soul-rest from the former servitude to its old propensities. Carnal nature, "the body of sin," having been destroyed, there is freedom from all the clamoring "lusts of the flesh." "But ye are not in the flesh, but in the Spirit; if so be the Spirit of God dwell in you."

8. This rest is one of *blissful assurance*. All doubt or uncertainty respecting the divine favor or the soul's salvation is excluded. "Perfect love casts out fear." "He that feareth is not made perfect in love." "The work of righteousness shall be peace, and the effect of righteousness, *quietness* and *assurance forever*." "Thou shalt keep him in perfect peace whose mind is stayed on Thee, because he trusteth in Thee."

9. This soul-rest is one of permanent assurance in respect to all our interests, temporal and eternal. If a blind son can trust his mother to prepare his food without the least fear of her poisoning him, or trust a father to lead him with as much confidence as the best eyes could inspire, may not the child of God trust the infinite love, power and wisdom of Christ? If a mother, father, wife or husband can be trusted without a disturbing doubt, may not a Christian rest in perfect repose upon the bosom of the God of truth and love?

10. This soul-rest is a state of *full satisfaction* in God as the changeless center of moral gravitation. "This God is my God forever and ever." The soul's chief good, "Whom have I in heaven but thee?" When our blessed Savior stood up and cried on the last great day of the feast: "If any man thirst, let Him come unto me and drink," He called upon all men to drink at the fountain of his own bound-

less felicity. He desires His children to enjoy what He enjoys. "My peace I give unto you." A peace like the ocean's depth, far beneath all storms and forever undisturbed. "These things have I spoken unto you, that my joy might remain in you, and that your joy might be full." This completes the climax. Christ's peace is full of mighty love and power. It was his *last*, his *best*, and his *dying* legacy to believers. "We which have believed do enter into rest."

This rest, or peace, cannot be perfect in the soul until all the discordant elements of indwelling sin are cleansed from the heart. Perfect purity precedes perfect peace. Perfect submission precedes perfect soul rest. Perfect love excludes all evil tempers. The fullness of the Spirit secures a subdued and regulated sensibility. "The fruit of the Spirit is love, joy, peace, longsuffering, gentleness, goodness, faith, meekness, temperance." Every believer is under obligation to God, to himself, and to the world to fully believe and enter into this rest without delay.

20
DIVINE VISITATIONS

WE HAVE HEARD OF "angels' visits." Though we have had no experience in this regard, yet we can easily conceive somewhat of what they are. What an era in our existence would such a visitation be! It would doubtless make us wiser and better during the remainder of our life.

But what must it be to have a visit from God! Who of us has had this experience? Who can tell what it is? There are some who have had this experience— *"Thou visitest him."* Those who have had these divine visitations can tell us something, though they cannot tell us all about them.

In such visitations, there is certainly a direct intercommunion of mind with mind, between the creature and God, of which the soul is just as conscious, as it is of its own operations. It is clear, from the Bible and from experience, that the soul may have certain and distinct apprehensions of the presence and manifestation of God. It is one thing for the soul to have apprehension that it is the constant object of omnific inspection, and a very different thing to have the high and lofty "One that inhabiteth eternity," descend to visit us in direct intercommunion with our minds—to be the conscious subjects of His blessed presence and communion. "I will draw *nigh* unto you." "Ye shall seek me and *find me.*" "*I will manifest myself unto you.*"

The effect of such divine visitations, is the most precious conceivable. In such the cup of blessedness is full. The river of life rises in the soul and bears it onward into an ocean of peace and blessedness where it finds neither shore nor bottom.

These visits have a transforming power upon the heart and character. New life and vigor are at once diffused throughout the soul. After these visits the mind has a sense of God's presence, and a realization of His truth and faithfulness, and such an assurance of His love as it never had before.

Reader, should your soul receive one such visitation you would be a new man the remainder of your earthly pilgrimage. In that visit you would learn more of God than you ever learned before; and your sense of His presence and perfections, and of the infinite fullness of His grace and love would become much more distinct and vivid.

You will then realize an entirely new relation to God in prayer. Then prayer to you will not be speaking to an impalpable, imaginary being, but to an omnipresent mind. You will know what it is to "speak to God face to face," and to plead with Him with an importunity, which His presence and grace alone can inspire. Then you will have "power with God," and His promises will be all "yea and amen in Christ Jesus."

The Bible will then become to you a new book. In reading it will seem the voice of God to your soul. It will become spirit and life, and a medium of communion with Him, in which you will behold, as in a glass, His image and glory.

Such visitations break the charm of this world, they

spoil earthly pleasures by fixing the soul's supreme delight on Christ and heavenly things. Christ becomes to the soul, "the rose of Sharon," "the lily of the valley," "the king in his beauty," "the brightness of the Father's glory," "the chief among ten thousand," and "the One altogether lovely." These visitations secure a religious standpoint, where the charming glories of "Immanuel, God with us," are poured upon the soul.

Such are some of the results of these divine visitations. If the reader asks, "On what conditions God will condescend to visit me?" we answer, "You must be humble and contrite in spirit, and tremble at the word of God." God must be sought with all the heart. With deep penitence and contrition for past transgressions, you must humble yourself before God, and by consecration and faith descend into the fountain of cleansing opened at Jerusalem "for sin and uncleanness," and there become "pure in heart." Then reader you will "see God." Then God will visit you. Then the Father will love you; He and Christ will come and make their abode with you.

Will you take this subject to your closet, and there think upon it, and pray over it in the presence of Him who is "mindful of the sons of men and *visits them*?" When He abides with you, and you continue in His love, "God will become your everlasting light, and the days of your mourning will be ended."

21
WALKING ALONE WITH JESUS

IT IS COMPARATIVELY an easy thing to be a Christian when the multitude bow in adoration at Jesus' feet, and it requires no great energy of spirit to consent to be identified with the followers of Christ, when the multitude follow, crying, "Hosanna to the Son of David." It was a very pleasant thing to be a disciple amid the beaming glories of the Mount of Transfiguration. But when we are required to follow Jesus, "without the camp, bearing the reproach," when the most of the world seem to have turned against him, that is quite another thing.

Almost any one can live religion in a time of general revival, when multitudes are rallying to the cross, and one seems almost irresistibly wafted along by the breath of prayer, and the burst of praise; but when the searching, trying, sifting time is come, it requires grace and nerve and sterling worth to stand the fire.

How pure and free the moral atmosphere that blows in gales of grace over our "feasts of tabernacles" in the leafy grove? How easy then to throw off all restraint, and with hearts refreshed and gladdened by showers of redeeming mercy, to worship God. Oft have we felt to exclaim, as we have mingled in these hallowed associations:—

> "My willing soul would stay,
> In such a frame as this,
> And sit and sing herself away,
> To everlasting bliss."

But these seasons do not always continue, a few brief days and the hundreds of happy faces that greet us are scattered far and wide. We must go out to grapple with stern realities. Difficulties soon loom in fearful array, testing our utmost fortitude and grace. We meet with little sympathy from the wicked world or from a faithless Church. The masses have no eyes to see the true beauties and importance of spiritual things—no heart to appreciate the workings of the Holy Ghost.

If in the fullness of our hearts, we seek to magnify the "riches of grace" by testifying how freely "the blood cleanseth," we may not expect universal credence in our testimony, nor universal sympathy with our position. Suspicious glances, and half suppressed (if not loudly proclaimed) opinions about "high professions," will indicate the popular sentiment, and teach us that there is something more than imagination in the idea of standing alone with Jesus.

We are social beings; and we easily see the tendency to mutual dependence in an unlawful degree. There is an important sense in which every disciple must stand and fight, and fall alone. The stupendous destinies of our immortal existence hang trembling over the decisions of our own individual will. Alone we must pass the shady valley of the tomb, and alone go up to receive the changeless sentence of our final Judge. God and our solitary souls will be the only parties.

We must walk alone with Jesus, and though human friendships should all be sundered, and the millions of earth should constitute one unbroken line of opposition, hurling the darts of hellish hate, and pouring out the bitterest anathemas on our heads, we are to walk alone with Jesus, and "smile at Satan's rage."

There is such a thing as being weaned from this delusive world, and shut up with God. Human sympathy may be sweetly soothing to our aching hearts, but it can never meet the deepest wants of our nature. In a very deep and peculiar sense we must be saved from each other and walk alone with Jesus.

22
THE CHRISTIAN PASTOR'S RESPONSIBILITIES

WHEN A PEOPLE RECEIVE a man who has been set apart to preach the gospel, and make him their spiritual watchman, placing him in their midst as a sentinel against impending danger, they lay on him solemn responsibilities. These responsibilities God lays upon every pastor, who, by his Providence and Spirit, he calls into any field of pastoral labor.

The spiritual pastor assumes the care of souls. The thousand influences which must affect their moral state he must study. He must know his people—not their names only, or their general character, or their place and weight in the social world, but he must know their moral state and history, and everything that affects their spiritual life and progress; else, how can he give each a portion in due season. How else can he be their spiritual guide?

Of the hundreds who constitute his charge, many are in youth, and he has the responsibility of guarding the influences under which their characters are formed for life and for eternity. The influences they exert upon each other—which help to develop their characters, and have much to do therewith—he must not sleep over.

A large number are more advanced in life, but are still in their sins. All the Sabbaths and sermons they have enjoyed; all the afflictions and all the mercies, and all the revivals they have passed through, have hitherto failed to subdue their hearts. They are only the more hardened. How often will the faithful pastor ponder their cases one by one, and ask himself what new means can he employ, or what new effort can he put forth by which lie may hope to reach each man's heart and conscience and save his soul.

There will be some in the bosom of the church, over whom his soul yearns with tenderest compassion, for he fears they have but a name to live. "Oh," he asks, "must I lead them again and again to the communion table, take their children in my arms and dedicate them to God, and follow them through the sick chamber to the grave, and have no more evidence than I now have, that they are God's children?" Alas! what a trial is this. How many a pastor's heart has ached under it!

Sometimes a pastor is summoned to the dying bedside of one of his charge, on whom the hand of God has fallen, and the dying man is in his sins. His heart would cry out, "Oh, if he might spare me the bitterness of this scene! Must I go and see a lost soul torn away from among my own people? Have I given him every warning that I might have given, and plied every means I could for his salvation as I should have done? Must he die under the displeasure of God, and must I meet him at the bar of God and answer there to the responsibilities of my pastorate?"

These are fearful responsibilities. When we see them in their full extent, and in their bearing on the world to come, no wonder we cry out, "Who is sufficient for these things?"

If there were not some redeeming and sustaining considerations, no man with his eyes open would ever assume such responsibilities as these. No wise man, without positive convictions of duty, would make himself liable to such pains and penalties for unfaithfulness. It involves such ceaseless cares, and trusts of such boundless magnitude, if there were not something to sustain and remunerate the pastor beyond the honor which men award, or the salary they pay—no man would be found to assume them.

But there is something beyond—infinitely beyond these inducements and supports. Jesus Christ has been a pastor himself watching for souls, and entering most wonderfully into their sympathies and wants. He knows the heart of the faithful pastor therefore, and will not be very far away when his soul yearns with parental and pastoral solicitude over immortal souls.

Christ has gone to his reward, and every faithful pastor shall receive his reward when he has finished his work; and besides, He will sustain and bless us in our work. The tears we shed, fall not unnoticed by him. The prayers and agonies and labors of the faithful minister shall not be in vain. They, like their Master, shall see of the travail of their soul and be satisfied.

Then let us, dear brethren, feel that while our work is arduous, it is also glorious; and though full of care and toil, it will be full of fruit to the glory of God.

23
"HAVE ANY OF THE RULERS BELIEVED ON HIM?"

THERE IS NO ROYAL WAY to the favor of God or to heaven. God is no respecter of persons. Human distinctions are mainly confined to man, and to this world, and human depravity has much to do with them.

The question at the head of this article, shows the rule by which some people judge of religion— "Have any of the rulers believed on Him?"

A due regard for the judgment and opinions of the great and the learned, we suppose no reasonable person will question, and, yet, too much dependence upon the opinions of great men, so-called, respecting the experimental truths of religion is not wise. There is a better, and a safer way. The Savior said— "If any man will do His will, he shall know of the doctrine, whether it be of God." We may know by experience, respecting Christian holiness, "whether any good thing can come out of Nazareth," "*Come and see.*"

The religion of our Lord Jesus Christ has been to a great extent rejected by the rulers of this world, nor has God especially consulted the wisdom, power and wealth of men in establishing His Church.

A life of mortification, self-denial, and humility does not comport with the inclinations of those who will have their portion in this life. Hence, it is no uncommon thing for those elevated in their relative position, and honored by men, to possess a strong repugnance to self-denial and full obedience to the will of God. Such a course comes in conflict with pride, dignity, self-importance, and love of applause. It is very natural for those in authority, or of noble birth, or possessed of wealth and rank to place a high estimate on themselves and disparage others. Such are inclined to be impatient under restraint or contradiction, and to imagine because they are great in some things, they are great and wise in all things. This is a very common mistake. We should be wise in our discrimination concerning the greatness of great men. Most of great men, are great only in some things, while in other things they are on a level with, or below mediocrity.

Evangelical obedience and faithfulness to God, necessitates a submissive, humble, childlike spirit. It was in view of these things, that Christ, declared His Father had hid many spiritual things "from the wise and prudent, and had revealed them unto babes," and the apostle— "Not many wise men after the flesh, not many mighty, not many noble, are called; but God hath chosen the foolish things of the world to confound the wise; and God hath chosen the weak things of the world to confound the things which are mighty; and base things of the world, and things which are despised, hath God chosen, yea, and things which are not, to bring to naught things that are; that no flesh should glory in His presence." Pride and contempt, standing in the way of candor, argument and truth, have kept many a man out of Christ.

The great mass of God's people have always been more

from the humble walks of life, than from the higher classes, or the elevated ranks of life. True virtue or excellence, sincerity and amiability, honesty and purity are usually found with those in humble life. Divine grace has been most displayed in reforming and purifying the lives of the common people and especially the ignorant, the vicious, the weak and the abandoned.

It has been no uncommon thing for the proud and haughty to oppose Christian holiness, by ridiculing its friends as poor, and ignorant, weak and credulous. Such people looking down with contempt upon the deluded Methodists, appear to overlook the fact, that God has great regard for the common people, the teachable, simple and humble, and out of this class has always selected most of those who have been His chosen instruments and His favored people.

No doctrine of Scripture depends for its success on human wisdom or greatness, and the prevalence and influence of Christian purity is not dependent on any class of men, high or low, great or small, rich or poor. Any religious system built on human power, wisdom, or wealth will be confounded and brought to naught. It is safe only to trust in God.

We seriously doubt that God is pleased with the sickening *toadyism*, so excessively developed in some of our Churches over *some supposed great ones.*

This thing appears to be growing among us, and is becoming to some of our sister Churches an occasion of amusement rather than strengthening their confidence in our good sense. Perhaps it would not hurt us as a Church to dispense with our toadyism entirely.

The truth of God, is alike adapted to all classes, and it has pleased our Heavenly Father, that the doctrine and experience of Christian holiness should commend itself to the most profound and lofty intellects, as well as to the common mass or ordinary sinners. He has raised up among our great men many devoted advocates and faithful witnesses of this grace.

The history of Methodism points out many of our chief ministers, whom the Church has delighted to honor, because they honored God with pure lives, and devotion to the doctrine of entire sanctification. Men who believed it, preached it, professed it, and lived it; and whose names are "as ointment poured forth," and many of them though dead, still speak through their works for it.

The Presidency of Wesleyan University has been especially blest with this class of men—Wilbur Fisk, Stephen Olin and Cyrus D. Foss.

What a trio of men of God! each through grace mighty in Christ, enjoying and standing as witnesses of full salvation.

Dr. Fisk was gloriously sanctified at old Eastham, and came back to the University, and walked with the sweetness of an angel until God took him. Dr. Olin sought a fullness in Christ, away in Italy, and lost self in an ocean of love, and confessed to his friends the great work of God in his soul. Bishop Foss has walked in the sunshine and sweetness of perfect love for years, and has often given his personal testimony to this precious grace. No minister coming from the sacred walls of Wesleyan University ought to give his trumpet any uncertain sound in this great central idea of the blessed Bible.

We could mention many in these days, who, have found this great treasure, and now stand among the strongest and most evangelical ministers in the Church of God.

God be praised! a still brighter day is yet to dawn upon the Church. The prejudice which has overshadowed this subject is being dispelled, and holiness must and will triumph. While God is raising up advocates of this grace from all classes, and in all Churches, let us not forget, our sole dependence is on Him.

No matter who embraces it, or otherwise, He is our dependence, and let us not glory in men.

24
THE DEATH OF SAINTS

"Precious in the sight of the Lord, is the death of His Saints."

WE ARE ACCUSTOMED TO speak of Death as "the king of terrors," and apart from the teachings of Revelation, we could not speak otherwise. God's word pours light into the dark grave, and while Christians are not exempt from the stroke of mortality, they are saved from the sting of death, which is sin.

God regards the death of saints with profound interest. "Precious in the sight of the Lord is the death of His saints." Death introduces the child of God into everlasting safety, purity and blessedness. The pious dead have run the race which was set before them, and reached the goal. They have fought the good fight, and the last struggle is over. The sword of the warrior is exchanged for the victor's crown. The little vessel, long tossed on the stormy sea of temptation and trial, has reached the haven, sheltered from every storm. The shock of corn is gathered into the heavenly garner. The sheep so long pursued by the devouring wolf, is now safely folded in the arms of the great Shepherd.

Probation is at an end. The flesh no longer lusts against the spirit, and the great battle of life is ended. The soul in heaven is established in holiness. No spot of guilt can ever defile its conscience again. Even the possibility of sinning is forever excluded. Each of the glorified bears the beautiful image and moral perfections of God, and all radiant with divine luster, will increase in glory forever. God dwells among his own, and "they serve him day and night in his temple." Their Sabbath never ends, and their worship never languishes. "The inhabitants" of that land "shall not say, I am sick." All tears shall be wiped away. "There shall be no more death, neither sorrow, nor crying; neither shall there be any more pain." "They shall hunger no more, neither thirst any more, neither shall the sun light on them, nor any heat; for the Lamb which is in the midst of the throne shall feed them, and shall lead them unto living fountains of water."

Heaven is the gathering place (the glorious home) of all who have followed Jesus on earth. What an innumerable host of friends and glorified saints are there! The harmony and bliss of heaven is never interrupted. No breath of slander shall ever taint that pure atmosphere; no fires of envy ever burn there; no deception, or treachery, or unkindness, wound or make bleeding hearts there! Misapprehension, ingratitude, coolness, doubt, and fear, are no more. Love, perfect and everlasting, shall reign in that bright world forever. To all this felicity, death is the gate of entrance. How precious. then, in the sight of the Lord, must be the death of his saints!

25
MINISTERS NEED THE HOLY SPIRIT

THE APOSTLES STUDIED THEOLOGY three years; Christ, the Great Teacher, was their professor, and still they were not prepared to proclaim "the glad tidings of great joy" until they had received a special baptism of the Holy Spirit for their work. They were held from their work, and commanded, "Not to depart from Jerusalem," but wait and pray for the needed and promised Spirit. It is quite as necessary now that ministers should receive the baptism of the Holy Ghost, before they go forth to their work.

This is seen in what is implied and included in the Spirit's baptism.

The Holy Spirit, in an important sense, is our *Teacher*. The Scriptures plainly declare that a prominent work of the Holy Ghost is to teach Christians, and "guide them into all truth." The Savior says, "The Holy Ghost shall teach you all things," "The Spirit of truth shall guide you into all truth." It is not necessary to a correct understanding of these, and similar passages, that we push them to the unwise extreme of assumed inspiration, or of superseding the need of the Bible. The Bible is the word of the Spirit, and is to be *illuminated* by the Spirit, but never superseded by it.

Humanity is so blind and dull of apprehension in respect to spiritual things, that stumbling and blundering are inevitable without the Spirit's illumination. Then, in our depravity, "The things of the Spirit of God (the truths revealed in the written Word) are foolishness unto them; they cannot know them because they are spiritually discerned." However much we may study the Bible, unless the Spirit illuminate us, we shall, in a measure at least, be "blind leaders of the blind."

The deep spiritual truths of the Gospel we can know only by the divinely illuminated word, and this is by the Holy Ghost as a spiritual teacher. He reveals no new truths, but opens to our understandings those already given in the inspired Bible. With our souls filled with the Spirit, we shall be full of light, and full of truth. A minister called of God to preach the Gospel, who is full of the Holy Spirit *is full of sermons*. Such know but little about *"grinding out sermons,"* they are full of them; the truth in them is like a well of water springing up continually.

We have a clear illustration of the foregoing, in the case of the Apostles, before and after Pentecost. How little they knew of the Gospel and of its spiritual import before Pentecost, and how much afterward. Before, how blind, how dull of apprehension, how full of erroneous notions. But afterwards, how their knowledge increased, and how clear their views of the plan of salvation. This was the work of the Holy Spirit. This is the very effect produced, in all ages, on all men, who are baptized with the Holy Spirit.

The Holy Spirit both *clarifies* our spiritual vision and *intensifies* the power of apprehended truth. He gives the mind more clear and vivid views of truth already apprehended. All Christians, in a measure at least, have the Spirit's light shed on their minds. They have, in a general way, at all times a notion of the nature and the guilt of sin, and the provisions of the Gospel. But frequently these truths exert scarcely any influence upon them. Let the Holy Spirit shed on these indistinct truths His hallowed light, and the mind will be roused to intense activity. The whole soul will be stimulated by a power and energy it never knew before.

With the power of the Holy Ghost, the soul is flooded with light, and the great truths of the Gospel become living realities. Jesus Christ and Him crucified, hell with its eternal ruin, heaven with its endless bliss, become positive, practical matters of fact. Such ministers realize the danger of the impenitent, and act accordingly. "They cease not to warn every one night and day with tears." They labor to save men from hell as they would to save them from a burning wreck.

26
THE VINE WITH ITS BRANCHES

OUR SAVIOR SETS FORTH in the xv. chapter of John the great principles and facts of the Christian life, and its duties, by the vine and its branches.

Will the reader please turn and carefully read the first eight verses of that chapter.

There are several important truths plainly taught in this apologue.

1st. According to this figure all Christians are branches in Christ. "I am the vine, ye are the branches." Hence, no man is a Christian who is not in Christ, and every man is a Christian who is in Christ. This relation is mutual—the branch is united to the vine, and the vine is united to the branch. "I in them, and thou in me."

2d. Christ stands in the same relation to the Christian, and the Christian to Christ, as the vine to the branches, and the branches to the vine. The Christian's life is in Christ, as the life of the branch is in the vine. The branch partakes of the nature of the tree, is nourished by its juice, and lives by its life; so the Christian, by abiding in Christ is made to partake of the divine nature, and has life in

Him. So intimate and vital is the relation between Christ and His members that they have one and the same life.

3d. No man remains a Christian any longer than he abides in Christ. "If a man abide not in me, he is cast forth as a branch, and is withered."

If the branch is severed it withers and dies.

4th. It teaches, that in order to continue in Christ—to remain Christian—we must bear fruit—must be useful. "Every branch in me, that beareth not fruit, He taketh away," If this teaches anything, it is, that we can only abide in Him by bearing fruit— "so shall ye be my disciples."

5th. It clearly teaches the possibility and liability of apostasy. The branches taken away must be real branches in the vine. If the Christian bear not fruit, he will incur a cutting off, which is real apostasy. As a vine-dresser will cut off all fruitless and dead branches, so Christ will take those away who bear no fruit. It is said here in the plainest manner, that a soul may be as truly united to Christ as a branch is to the vine, and yet on account of unfruitfulness be cut off. No man can cut off a branch from a vine to which it never was united.

6th. Those who abide in Christ and bear fruit, He purgeth them—purifies them, that they may bear more fruit. That is, in the regenerate believer, who is a "branch in" Christ, and who "beareth (some) fruit," there remains impurity to be "purged" in order to greater fruitfulness.

Note. "The branch" is "in Christ;" and "If any man be in Christ, he is a new creature," and he "beareth fruit." He is therefore a true Christian, and a fruitful Christian, and yet God purgeth him. There is then in every such branch—in every such Christian something to be purged away; something of moral evil and defilement, that limits or hinders fruitfulness and needs extermination. Its removal is the work of God. *"He purgeth it."*

7th. This shows that corruption may yet remain in those

who are in Christ. After God purgeth it, He says, "Now are ye clean through the Word which I have spoken unto you," i.e., Christians are made clean through the purifying power of Christ's "Word." Hence the prayer of Christ— "Sanctify them through Thy truth."

8th. Christians sanctified by Christ and made clean, glorify God in bearing "much fruit." Increased fruitfulness is a result of cleansing, and an evidence of being cleansed. God is glorified proportionately to the quality, permanency, and abundance of Christian fruitfulness. Purity involves this. "Being made free from sin, ye have your fruit unto holiness."

This is natural, and reasonable; and finds plenty of analogies in nature. The sap of the vine alone can enable the branch to bear fruit. Right tempers spring alone from Christ, and right tempers only can produce right actions. Purity affords the graces of the Spirit a most luxuriant growth, bearing the fruit of righteousness to the praise and glory of God. Hence, "If a man therefore purge himself from these, he shall be a vessel unto honor, sanctified and meet for the Master's use."

27
THE BLISS OF THE PURIFIED

IN THE SOUL cleansed from all sin, all the fruits and graces of the Spirit exist complete in quality. Purity of heart implies grace without mixture, exclusive of all alloy—free from all its antagonisms in the soul.

Pure love is exclusive. It fills the soul and excludes all hatred, ill will, animosity, bitterness, clamor and wrath. It excludes all that class of vile and degrading passions, which are the chief elements of human corruption and woe.

When cleansed, the heart is free from all pride, lusts, envy, jealousy, covetousness, impatience, and all unsanctified uneasiness and fear. Purification not only extirpates all vile and disturbing evils, but secures an unobstructed development of all the moral excellencies implanted in the soul at regeneration. Holiness has both a negative and a positive aspect; the heart is both cleansed from sin and filled with love. There is both an extermination and an impartation. Inbred sin is exterminated, and the Holy Spirit has full possession of the soul. Praise the Lord!

In the purified soul, faith has reached a measure of strength, excluding unbelief, doubts and uncertainty.

"Meridian light puts doubt to flight."

Hence, the soul easily, peacefully and confidingly abides in Christ. In Him, it has "wisdom, righteousness, sanctification and redemption." It has rest, satisfaction and salvation! "Bless the Lord, O my soul!" Salvation now! Salvation with no uncertainty! Salvation free and full! Salvation sweet and powerful! Salvation to the extent of the soul's present necessity—from both the guilt and the pollution of sin! Scriptural and evangelical salvation—both negative and positive—freedom from the condemnation of sin, the commission of sin and from the impurity of sin; with the possession of the graces of the Spirit, and the truth, "as it is in Jesus."

Some say, "entire sanctification is only a little more religion." True, it is more religion; but thank the Lord! it is more religion in "a clean heart." It is more religion with inbred sin or remaining impurity exterminated, and in this, the distinction exists, between merely getting more religion indefinitely and being entirely sanctified. A man may get more religion many times without having his soul fully cleansed from all sin.

"Blessed are the pure in heart." How rich, and how blessed this unmixed and powerfully intensified religious life. With such, the precious work of regeneration and all its concomitants are more manifest in the consciousness of the soul. They are more clearly apprehended, and more powerfully felt as solid, precious heart-felt realities. Holiness secures clearness of spiritual vision; or at least, a clearer apprehension of spiritual things, than can be otherwise obtained. "They shall see God."

"If we walk in the light, as He is in the light, we have fellowship one with another, and the blood of Jesus Christ,

His Son, cleanseth us from all sin." This "walking in the light" (in the light of truth and spiritual things), "as God is in the light." How delightful! How luminous and inspiring! How blessed!

Grace in a pure heart has advantages which it cannot have in the soul not wholly cleansed. When fully saved, there is a clearness, a freeness, a sweetness and fullness not possible in the mixed moral condition of the merely regenerate. Glory! and praise to our blessed Savior, He can and does save most gloriously when the soul is fully committed to Him, and His will is fully done.

It is no fault of Christ's that there are not to-day in the ministry of the Methodist Episcopal Church, fifteen thousand "mighty men of God," entirely sanctified and filled "with peace in believing, and joy in the Holy Ghost," engaged in the good work of "spreading scriptural holiness over these lands."

It is no fault in the rich and ample provisions of grace, that we have not now, in our own loved communion, fifty thousand class leaders filled with every spiritual benediction, Carvosso like, prepared to lead their little flocks into the "green pastures and beside the still waters."

It is no fault of the great atonement, or of our interceding Christ, nor of the blessed Bible, nor of the infinite and eternal Spirit, that we have not three millions of "wholly sanctified" Methodists on this continent moving with the tread of a moral earthquake, in evangelizing this world to God.

O, that I could utter all my soul on this subject in the ears of a thousand ministers, ten thousand class leaders, and ten times ten thousand Church members, all of whose prayers, sacrifices and tears should have reference to this world's salvation.

O, how desirable to have "perfect love," which "casts out fear," that makes us "free indeed," and secures within us a well of living water "springing up into everlasting life." To have all the mind that was in Christ, to be clothed in raiment bleached white in the Redeemer's blood, and to know something of the nature of that purity, which constitutes a chief element of paradise. O yes, yes, my inmost soul responds, yes!

There is such light, such love, such plainness, such certainty, such simplicity, such life, such power, such sweetness, such security, such divinity and glory wrapped up in the experience of a pure heart, as to make it joyful and desirable beyond all power of description.

I know this, dear reader. I would not dare to write it if I did not know it. O, this spiritual Kingdom! May the Lord help us to enter it more fully, so as to see and enjoy more of its charming glories. "Praise God from whom all blessings flow." Here we can find in abundant fullness, righteousness, peace and joy in the Holy Ghost."

Believe me, dear reader, our Methodist Canaan of perfect love is an exceeding goodly land.

28
THE JOY OF SALVATION

THE PSALMIST PRAYED — *"Restore unto me the joy of Thy salvation."* Ps. li.

Let me present a few elements of the joy of every truly saved soul.

1st. *There is a joy of pardon.*

All believers are forgiven, their sins are blotted out, they are justified freely and fully "through the redemption in Christ Jesus." The truly saved have a revelation made to them that God has forgiven all their sins, so that they possess the joy of pardon.

2d. *There is a sense of Divine reconciliation.*

The convicted sinner is made to realize that God is pleased with him, and he finds himself pleased with God. The moral estrangement between his soul and God has ceased. His opposition to God and shyness of Him has ended, and there is fellowship and friendship with Christ.

3d. *There is the joy of spiritual life.*

The Christian is quickened into a new spiritual life, full of sweetness, vitality and joy. It is the highest and most blissful form of life — the life of Christ in the soul, and the beginning of eternal life with all its beatitudes.

4th. *There is the spirit of love.*

"The love of God is shed abroad in the heart by the Holy Ghost." "Every one that loveth is born of God and knoweth God." This spirit is the fulfillment of the law, the root and foundation of all acceptable obedience. It is a sweet controlling force in the soul, existing both as a principle and as an emotion, involving *choice* and *delight* in God.

5th. *There is a sense of inward purity.*

This is partial or complete, as the soul is only regenerated, or entirely sanctified. Those but partially purified have some discordant element of indwelling sin to mar their peace, while those fully saved can say, with David Brainard, "I am clean from both past and present sin." When the blood of Christ has been applied to the heart, and the pure love of God fills the heart, there is a sweet sense of present inward purity.

"O the bliss of the purified."

6th. *There is a sense of inward harmony*—soul-rest.

The saved soul is in harmony with God, with all holy things, and with itself. Its powers are so purified, adjusted, and brought into such correlations with each other, and with God, that their action becomes *harmonious*. There is freedom from all discord in the soul. Grace attunes the soul to the sweet harmony of love by putting every pipe, string and active force in unison with Christ. O the bliss of being in *spiritual tone*, so that the Word and the Holy Ghost may produce the very harmony of heaven in our souls. When every power, every affection, and every element of the soul's activities is in such tune that not a note, not even a semi-note is out of harmony. *O what music!* No words can describe it. "*Joy unspeakable and full of glory.*"

7th. *There is a deep and solid sense of peace.*

Peace is an all-pervading element in the redeemed soul. "The Lord will give His people peace." God desires His children to enjoy what He enjoys, hence He says, "My peace I give unto you." When our blessed Savior stood and cried, "If any man thirst, let him come unto me and drink," He called upon all to come and drink at the fountain of His own infinite felicity. "These things have I spoken unto you (said He) that my joy might remain in you, and that your joy might be full."

8th. *There is a sense of blessed vision.*

Saints have been brought "out of darkness into light," and are "children of light." Their path is "as the shining light, that shineth more and more unto the perfect day." Light is the medium of sight. Grace reveals God. "Blessed are the pure in heart, for they shall see God." Pardon and purity place the soul where it apprehends God, where it sees the "King in His beauty," and where the charming glories of the God-man are poured upon the soul. The increasing vision of God and truth is a source of rapturous delight to every faithful child of God.

9th. *There is a joyous sense of blessed hope.*

Hope is the pleasing anticipation of future good. Every saint of God is begotten unto a lively hope, by the resurrection of Christ from the dead, to an inheritance incorruptible, undefiled, and that fadeth not away, and reserved in heaven for him. This hope is like an anchor to the soul, *sure* and *steadfast*. It is based upon the promise and oath of God, is sealed and witnessed to by the blood and death of Christ, and is as grand and glorious as heaven.

Remarks:

1. It is a fearfully ominous fact, that multitudes of professing Christians appear to be entirely destitute of religious joy — "the joy of the Lord."

2. A great many professors of religion seem not to care for this blessing, apparently forgetting that this joy is *inseparable from a truly religious life.*

3. It must appear that the absence of these elements of

religious joy negative a positively religious life.

Pardon, reconciliation, life, love, purity, soul harmony, peace, light and hope constitute the very essence of godliness.

4. Thousands of people who claim to be Christians are scrambling after dress, money and pleasure, running to concerts, shows, theaters, and parties of pleasure, while the closet, the prayer service and God are neglected.

5. Respecting all these pleasure-loving, wretched, muttering, grumbling professors, we feel like adopting the language of the Church of England, "*Good Lord deliver us.*"

6. The absence of spiritual joy dishonors God, and is a reproach to the religion of Jesus Christ. It is a great stumbling block to sinners, and leads them to think religion is a mere pretense—a sham.

Again, I pray from *legalists* and that *legal state of mind*, which underestimates, disparages and misrepresents religion, "*Good Lord deliver us.*"

29
REGENERATION WITH ITS CONCOMITANTS

IT IS FREQUENTLY SAID, the advocates of entire sanctification minify the grace and work of regeneration to make a place for entire sanctification. This is a mistake and a misrepresentation. The fact is, no class of Christian teachers emphasize more, or teach more clearly and fully all the essential items of initial salvation, including pardon or justification; regeneration or the new birth, the reception of spiritual life and heirship to eternal life, than those who teach the duty and privilege of being entirely cleansed from sin, and fully sanctified to God. They hold regeneration, with its accompaniments of pardon, adoption, dethronement of sin, and initial purification, as the greatest thing God ever does for a soul in this world, or any other. We believe with Richard Watson— "Regeneration, which accompanies justification, is a large approach to this state of perfect holiness."

Justification, regeneration and adoption, all things considered, are much greater than the purification of the child of God from remaining indwelling sin, which completes the work of entire sanctification.

Dr. Adam Clarke says, "justification is far greater than sanctification." After describing entire sanctification, he adds, "Great as this work is, how little, humanly speaking is it, when compared with what God has already done for thee." (See Clarke's Theology, p. 206.)

Justification and regeneration, including our change to the divine government and law, and the change wrought in us, are much greater than that of "perfect holiness," or our entire sanctification. In a judicial point of view, no change can exceed that which occurs when God pardons our sins, and the "washing of regeneration," which carries the soul back to the condition of childhood, involves the larger part of our purification. While this grace does not remove or destroy original or birth sin (so called), it does remove all our acquired depravity with its pollution. The declaration of Christ, "Except ye be converted and become as little children, etc.," throws a flood of light on this subject.

The *phenomenal*, or conscious experience of some who are entirely sanctified may sometimes appear greater than their regeneration, nevertheless with many, even this is not the case. Some with the flaming, glowing experience of purity, in the all cleansing blood of Christ, may have made the impression that the new birth and their initial salvation, was a small thing compared with the fuller cleansing in entire sanctification, but that was only in their emotional condition and gospel freedom.

Entire sanctification, as a moral condition, is only greater than regeneration, in that there is added to all that initial salvation includes, a complete cleansing of the soul, so that those great, grand initial facts which are coetaneous with the Christian life, stand out in the soul's apprehension of consciousness more clearly and intensely than ever. Hence it is that some are never fully satisfied with the evidence of their sonship and Christian character until their heart is fully cleansed. Full salvation sheds a flood of light on the regenerate and justified state.

O! for the light of purity to settle the minds of millions as to their justification.

30
SOME ENTIRELY SANCTIFIED IN ALL DENOMINATIONS

THERE HAVE BEEN holy men and women, entirely sanctified, in all ages, in all nations and in all Christian churches. While it is a lamentable fact, that a large proportion of Christian professors in the various churches deny the doctrine through misapprehension, prejudice or other causes, it must be conceded that many in all our sister denominations really trust the cleansing blood, and are pure-hearted Christians. They may not call their gracious state "perfect love," or "holiness," or "entire sanctification."

Many of these, if they were "taught the way of God more perfectly," would declare with John, "Herein is our love made perfect" and we would hear them exhort their brethren, saying, "It is the will of God even your sanctification," and "Therefore—let us go on unto perfection."

These pure-hearted believers, usually express their attainments by the terms "faith of assurance," "full assurance," "the higher life," and similar phrases which they think less offensive in their churches than "Christian perfection," "perfect love," and "sanctification," which as we view it, are more Scriptural, and are expressively significant of the work wrought. We are sorry to know that some of our ministers and members in like manner are adopting terms of their own in the place of the divinely inspired terms of the Bible.

In all periods of the Church, while there has been much darkness regarding the theory of gospel holiness, there have been beautiful examples of its possession. Many of the martyrs triumphed in this grace, in dungeons and at the stake who may have been very erroneous in their religious theory respecting this doctrine, as well as regarding many other doctrines.

Light has increased in the Church, and we are now ashamed of many superstitious absurdities once held in the earlier and darker days of our dispensation, and especially of early Roman and Protestant Christianity. What absurd and foolish notions were held by some very pious and great men regarding the doctrine of predestination, election and reprobation only a few years ago! There are very few now in any church who will teach all the sentiments of Calvin. The Antinomianism of the times of Wesley is fading away now as compared with bygone years.

So, with the doctrine of entire sanctification as set forth in the blessed Bible, it has been misunderstood and misrepresented and by many rejected; but with increasing light in the Church the crudities which have been thrown around it will disappear, and it will be more and more understood, and the churches will become more and more harmonious regarding its essential items and experience. In a few years there will come to be as much harmony regarding Christian sanctification as there is now regarding the doctrine of justification by faith.

31
HOLINESS IS RELIGION MADE EASY

WITH CHRISTIAN PURITY established in the soul, how easy and natural it is to love and obey God! Surely the devil has not all the advantage in this world. With the soul fully saved and full of peace, light and love, a religious life becomes second nature and a luxury; more of a divine charm than a tedious service.

The best religious life is the easiest life, and the hardest and most difficult one is a half-hearted one. A soul full of love delights in the law of God, and to such the divine commandments are never grievous but joyous. The law of sin and death, no more wars in his members, this being taken away he runs the way of God's commandments and finds them health and life to his soul.

The fully sanctified soul, like his blessed Master, is swallowed up in divine love and zeal, and it is his "meat and drink to do the will of his heavenly Father." To such a Christian God is his all in all. And whether he eat or drink, sleep or rest, labor, read, hear, speak or pray, whatever he does, he does all in the name of the Lord Jesus and to the glory of God. His eye is single and his whole body is full of light. His motives, disposition and desires are pure and right, and his life is hid with Christ in God. He lives by faith on the Son of God. His spiritual vision is clear and his communion with God unintermittent. He thinks, talks and acts with the full enjoyment of gospel holiness. He does not sin against God in thought, word and deed, as some profess to do, but honors God in thoughts, words and deeds.

Entire sanctification is a moral condition in which faith continually sees him that is invisible; a humility that pervades the soul as a subdued temper; a love that rules the heart as a sweet, heavenly disposition; a patience that calmly endures whatever God sends or allows; a submission that says in all things, "Not as I will, but as thou wilt"; a meekness that is undisturbed by fits of anger; a contentment that is happy in the allotments of providence; a gratitude that responds to divine beneficence; a courage that is invincible in the line of duty; a self-denial that takes pleasure in the will of God; a charity that puts the most favorable construction on everybody that the facts will justify; a peace like a river in depth and plenitude; a joy like a perpetual spring, and often "unspeakable and full of glory"; a hope like an anchor of the soul, sure and steadfast; a brotherly kindness that does to others as we would have done to us, and a purity that keeps all the passions and appetites in harmony with the will and law of God. All this becomes natural and easy.

32
WHY GOD DELAYS ANSWER TO PRAYER

THE PROPHET HABAKKUK two thousand five hundred years ago, under the pressure of spiritual need, cried to God: "O Lord, how long shall I cry, and thou wilt not hear! even cry out unto thee of violence, and thou wilt not save!" The question suggested by these words is, Why does not God more readily answer prayer? Very likely there are many reasons why prayer does not more generally receive immediate answer.

It may be because so many fail to see the plague, or spiritual ailments of their own hearts. Acceptable prayer must come from a heart sensible of its individual iniquities, and that lies in the dust, with humility before God. When the heart, conscious of its defilement, and humbled on its account, supplicates with "strong crying and tears," God will hear, and lift him up, and enable him to come boldly to the throne of grace, and obtain mercy and find grace to help in every time of need. The hindrance to successful prayer is never with God, but always with or in ourselves. "Ye ask and receive not, because ye ask amiss."

Delays in answer to prayer may be occasioned by littleness of prayer. He who prays but little or seldom, disobeys God—and he will not hear him when he does pray. We are commanded to pray without ceasing, and to pray with all prayer and supplication. He who prays but little not only displeases God, and grieves his Spirit, but loses the spirit of prayer—and he fails to pray effectually or fervently. It is the effectual and fervent prayer of the righteous that availeth much.

The delay in receiving answers in many instances may result from a lack of dependence upon Christ. God can hear and answer our prayers only through Christ; and when we fail to feel our dependence upon his merits and intercession, we pray in vain. God answers prayer for Christ's sake, and Christ is the only way of access to the throne of grace. The name of Christ may be used in our approaches to God from mere habit; when this is the case, our prayers will receive no answer. Delays in answer to prayer may result from a disobedient life. Disobedience blocks the work of God, and puts an embargo on the whole religious life. If we would have God hear and answer our prayers more readily, we must obey him more fully. He pays no man a premium for disobedience. Disobedience cuts the sinews of faith, and renders evangelical faith impossible; as conscious confidence (faith) and conscious rebellion cannot co-exist. One excludes the other. It should never be forgotten that the faith that justifies, sanctifies, and saves men, is inseparable from an obedient spirit. God hath joined them together, and no man can put them asunder. Acceptable prayer without faith is impossible, and faith without an obedient spirit is impossible. When our prayers are examined in the light of the inspired word of God, it is not difficult to see why so few are answered, and why our loving heavenly Father delays to bestow much that is sought at his hand. When Christians see the plague of their own hearts— when they are willing to fully obey God—when they pray without ceasing and stop trusting in means and measures and when they properly feel their dependence upon Christ, then God will hear and answer and pour them out a blessing that there shall not be room enough to receive it.

33
THE BLESSEDNESS OF PURITY

IT IS A REMARKABLE FACT that mankind, so universally in quest of happiness, searches for it in every place but the right one. They ransack creation to find it; while it lies beyond the bounds of creation.

The benevolent Creator, however, has made happiness possible to every creature—has brought it to our doors, has poured it upon us through a thousand channels, and we resist it through our perverse wills and misplaced affections, and remain ill at ease when we might be rejoicing in God our Savior.

That life is fraught with ills, no observer of society can doubt. "In the world ye shall have tribulation." But how shall these ills—these destroyers of our happiness—be removed, and their power broken? To meet this desideratum, we might propose several rules in detail, which would all be very good; but it will be a shorter method to point the soul to that holiness, without which we cannot see God, which affords an adequate, many-sided remedy for them all; that touches the core of the difficulty, and sends health and comfort through the whole soul. It gives content in the palace and the dungeon; in the sunlight of prosperity, and in the dark day of sorrow and adversity.

Holiness brings man to the true source of happiness, which is God. Most men are miserable because they expect happiness from the wrong source. They look where it cannot be found, and hence must be disappointed. The sage has taught us that "Man wants but little, nor wants that little long;" but the great study and mistake of man has been to add to his list of wants *ad infinitum*. The higher gift eclipses the lower, so that in a sense the holy man realizes but one indispensable want. Others may be well, but he can do without them; only God is necessary.

Holiness promotes human happiness by affording a true estimate and interpretation of the ills of life. These ills, to many, so embitter the cup as to render life uncomfortable, and cause the sweets that are mingled with it to be unappreciated. To the good man, though severe and often crucifying, yet they appear but for a moment. And during the moment of their continuance, instead of a curse, they afford lessons of wisdom, and work out a far more exceeding and eternal weight of glory. The pure heart is meek and resigned, and extracts sweetness out of the most bitter tribulation. It even marshals the dark messengers of earthly sorrow into the line of helpers in the way to heaven.

Holiness imparts stability to character, and enables the soul to stem the tide of tribulation without vexing the soul, or fretting away its meekness, faith or patience. Most that fall at all, fall by littles. They lose a little patience here, and a little meekness there, and a little faith yonder, until they find one day that their religion has mysteriously departed. Holiness gives a man ballast, and staidness of life, and carries him safely through the petty vexations which lie along his path.

Holiness preoccupies the mind with controlling and

elevating thoughts of God and heaven. We are made to think, but not on trifles. The soul without grace is inclined to turn in upon itself, upon the little cares and vexations of life, and so consume its own energies by chafing and fretting, as to bring along gray hairs before their time. We are bidden to look up. The martyr, we are told, while gazing on the ineffable glories of Christ, forgot the fires kindling about his poor body.

There are moments of leisure, or weakness, or sickness, when the trials and ills of life rush in like a flood, and the worldly man has no standard to lift against them. Who has not felt the need of Divine and superhuman help in the hour of greatest weakness and trial; when these ills pelt us unmercifully like a legion of devils, determined on our ruin? All who would live safely and happily in this world should seek, first and last, to be holy. "Blessed are the pure in heart."

34
How to Preach Well

A DISTINGUISHED DIVINE, of great heavenly-mindedness, left on record this resolution: "Always to eat my sermons before I preach them." This resolution we both approve and love. It commends itself to our reason and to our heart. It breathes the spirit of profound sincerity, and evinces a heart that dealt with truth honestly.

When a man delineates spiritual religion, not so much as the result of study and reasoning, as a matter of his own experience; when he unfolds it with that spirit of life and earnestness which accompany truth drawn from one's own bosom, he cannot be powerless. There is nothing vague and uncertain, nothing unintelligible, in the speech of such a man.

His heart's desire is that his hearers may be saved. He presses earnestly towards his object. His inward emotion he cannot conceal. It bursts from the lips; it speaks from the eye; it modulates the tone; it pervades the whole manner; it possesses and controls the whole man; he is seen to be in earnest; he disarms criticism; he convinces, he persuades, he speaks with power.

A pure life, harmonizing with the truth we preach, puts all the human faculties under the pressure and power of sanctified motives. When the heart is pressed and well-nigh crushed with a sense of its duty and responsibility, then it will speak with power; then the heart and conscience will exert their combined power, and every talent will be employed, and the whole man is urged into full and efficient action.

How often have we felt the conviction forced upon us that this or that brother did not eat his sermon before he preached it, or, if he did, he failed to digest it, or reduce it to practice afterwards.

We have sometimes wished that in some favored moment, when the heart is most tender, and most open to kind, admonitory suggestions, we could get a secret audience with such a brother. We would feel constrained, perhaps, to say to him: "My brother, are you not conscious that the tone of piety which the spirit of your sermon breathes is very much higher than that which you exhibit on all other occasions, except when preaching? Do you not in your public instructions hold up a standard of life which you neither attain, nor seem honestly to seek to attain yourself? Do you not urge a measure of self-denial which you do not practice; and a fervency in prayer to which your own closet never bears witness, and a zeal for the salvation of souls which is not apparent in yourself when out of the pulpit?"

We know these are tender points; but are they not of the most vital importance? Can we expect that the truth from our lips will be like a two-edged sword, unless it be sustained by a godly life, enforcing the conviction on saint and sinner, that we are radically honest, and profoundly sincere in all we say and teach?

If it be not so with us, our hearers will say, "Oh, he does not mean much! You know he does not himself live as he says we all should; it is his profession to preach, and he must be smart, or the church would not like him." Now, when the most eloquent and logical preaching under heaven is counteracted by this undercurrent from the preacher's known spirit and life, what power can there be in his utterances, or what good can he do? Nay, what evil will he not do?

Alas! the fearful effects of making religion and its teachings a *professional* thing, and abstracting from this profession the heart's deep honesty and realization of the truth taught. It will never do to make sermon-making a science, and preaching a profession, with the vitality of godliness wanting. Such a course will make more infidels than Christians.

"Thou therefore who teachest another—teachest thou not thyself?" If we fail to do this, our hearts will wax hard, and the Spirit of God will forsake us. All ministerial efficiency is of God. With his smiles and presence, with his all-powerful aid, they can do anything; without it, just nothing, or really what is worse than nothing. Without God with us, we may preach so as to harden men's hearts, but not so as to subdue and save them—this requires the might of God's Spirit.

No man has a right to expect that God will be in his words if God is not in his heart and life. If there is that in our heart and life which displeases the Holy Ghost, how can we expect him to sanction our preaching, and put the seal of heaven upon our mission? God never winks at sin.

All unbelief makes God a liar. All worldliness is an abomination in his sight, and anything that shuts out the spirit of God from a preacher's heart renders his preaching powerless.

35
THE SELF-PERPETUATING POWER OF SIN

Every one must see that it is an awful fact, if true, that sin has in its own nature a self-perpetuating power. That this is true, we have too many and too painful evidences.

So far as we know, there are but two races of beings who have ever made trial of the energies of sin upon the minds of moral agents—fallen angels and fallen men. The angels that kept not their first estate, began with one sin. Having committed that, it became a momentous question—all heaven hung in suspense to know the result; will they go on and commit another, and another? The question was soon decided, and decided so as to banish all doubt of their future course. They went on sinning. The first step led the way to the second. Each successive sin made a perpetual course of sinning the more certain. Each sin made a fresh impression on their moral powers, and that impression served only to obliterate more perfectly every tendency toward holiness, and confirm every tendency toward sin. Hence, they went on with a continually increasing momentum.

So with sinning man. If we could see his case developed without any restraint from God's providence or from his Spirit, we have every reason to suppose that it would not differ in the least from the case of fallen angels. None would return to virtue or the path of life. Every new step forward would make the return more hopeless, and the onward and downward movement more rapid and more desperate. Such are all the tendencies of sin, and we see it clearly developed in these awful cases which bear the marks of a soul abandoned of God.

Fix your eye on the drunkard who has gone beyond the restraints of his honor, his wife, his children, his health, his soul. See his motions. Mark his recklessness. If no strong arm interposes, will he return to sobriety? Never! You feel safe in predicting his swift and hopeless ruin.

Let your eye run along the track of that young man who went into the city for a place behind the counter. Once honest, moral, diligent, in a dark moment the tempter came. He gambled, he defrauded, or he set his foot within the door of "her whose house is the way to hell, going down to the chambers of death." The first step demanded the second. He must cover up, for how can he bear the disgrace of such a sin. Hence the thousand arts of concealment, and no longer any shrinking from falsehood. This serves to crush the self-restoring vitality of his moral system. And there is that forbidden sweet; he has sipped the cup of pleasure; it maddens his soul and he dashes on. Ah, he is as good as dead already! Satan has his fetters riveted on, and leads him captive at his own will.

Oh, it is a fearful thing to sin! It so paralyzes the power of virtuous principles, quickens the susceptibility to temptation, hedges up the way of the sinner's return—commits him to one invariable course, onward and downward, maddening the soul for still darker deeds, and more damning guilt. This is the great secret of the fearful deeds of wickedness so prevalent in these days.

35: The Self-Perpetuating Power of Sin

Verily, sin is no trifle. Who would dare begin if he saw where it would end! Who would put his bark even in the outer and gentle sweep of the maelstrom for the pleasure of floating without oar or sail, if he clearly saw the certain acceleration of his velocity, the hopelessness of return, and the rocks at the fatal center, where hope and life are dashed forever?

Reader, there is for sinners on this earth only one remedy—the almighty arm of Jesus. Cry to him and he will save; he has saved myriads; and do this as soon as you can. Every moment's delay gives you a more fearful momentum in sin; draws you nearer the vortex of ruin, and places you still farther away from the outstretched arm that alone can save you. He that believes and does accordingly, shall be wise for himself; but whoso scorns, or passes by in neglect, he alone must bear it.

36
"THE SWORD OF THE LORD AND OF GIDEON"

Has not "the set time come to favor Zion?" The revival fire is now burning in more than a thousand churches in our land. God is marvelously at work. The flame is spreading. Multitudes are being converted to Christ. Many of our sanctuaries are being made vocal with the songs and praise of new born souls. Everlasting praise, be unto the Father, the Son and the Holy Ghost.

Shall the work cease? And as a church are we all ready for this "coming of the Lord?" As soldiers of Christ, are we in the field, and each at his post?

If any of the professed friends of Jesus are not ready for this blessed visitation, let us humble ourselves before God. Let us search our hearts, and by prayer, fasting, supplications and faith, press into the inner temple—the holy of holies.

Let us go to God in our closets, and there on our knees repent, confess, consecrate and believe until our hearts are melted, subdued, and wholly sanctified to God. Let us plead in the dust until we get the victory, the mighty working spirit. Then for a general shout, "the Sword of the Lord and of Gideon."

This is a special time to work for God. O! that every dear follower of Christ may know "the day of their visitation." Let the Gospel invitation become common on the lips of all Christians— "come thou with us and we will do thee good, for the Lord hath spoken good concerning Israel." Husbands, look after your unconverted wives. Wives, be true and faithful to your unsaved husbands. Christian parents, do all your duty to your unconverted children, and put forth a wise and timely effort to save them now. Dress them, educate them, and train them for God and immortality. Let every Christian go out after his unconverted neighbor, and be perseveringly faithful to them.

Let the great cry be, Lord, send a general baptism throughout the whole church, that there may be a united engagement east and west, north and south, mighty for God.

Let us give for God, and work for God, and never mind the noise or excitement of the battle, but stand with united sympathies, prayers and co-operation against the infernal allies, "the world, the flesh, and the devil." Some wise ones, and some popular, fashionable, modernized professors will cry out against excitement and extravagance; but let God's people fear nothing but sin, and rest assured the Lord will take care of his own work and work in his own way. If we would have the altar fires of Heaven kindled everywhere, and this revival flame spread all through our land, we must labor for it. We must pray for it. We must believe for, and expect it, and may God grant it. Amen!

O that I could utter all my soul on this subject, to fifty thousand Methodist class-leaders, in our own loved church. Come, friends of our mighty Savior, in his name and strength let us do all our duty now. Time flies. Let us begin at once. Seize the present and do today the work of today. God help you to begin now! This moment. Don't let the membership fail to pray for the ministry, that they may be filled with the Holy Ghost, and wield "the sword of the spirit, which is the word of God." Oh! that this Jerusalem blade divinely furbished and furnished, may be made bare in achieving great and glorious victories, filling heaven with joy and hell with consternation. With over fifteen thousand traveling Methodist ministers in our division of the grand army, the battle ought to wax hot, and multitudes of the ungodly ought to be "pricked in the heart," and lead to cry for mercy. O that "the slain of the Lord may be many." Fellow soldiers, and brethren beloved, in the strength of the God of battles let us buckle on the armor and rally to the field of conflict, and let us make one long and mighty onslaught upon selfishness, pride, covetousness, infidelity and every other power of hell.

Brethren, if there is a heaven and a hell, a God and Savior, a divine law, unalterable and eternal, let us see to it that we are doing our whole duty now.

37
THE ATONEMENT

THERE ARE THREE THINGS bearing directly on this great truth, which I know with the most satisfactory assurance. The first is that I am a sinner and need pardon The second is that my nature is polluted and needs cleansing. The third is the precious fact, that through faith in Christ, I have, and do obtain *pardon* and *purity*.

The first and second I know by direct conscious-ness — or conscious experience. Of the third, I have no less satisfactory and certain assurance, being promised in the revealed truth of God, witnessed to by the Holy Spirit, and realized by conscious experience.

Very likely I know little about the *nature* of the atonement, or the manner in which the death of Christ lays an adequate foundation for justification and sanctification.

As a foundation of faith, however, I ask no other consideration, in connection with a consciousness of my necessities, than the plainly revealed fact that God can be just, and justify the believer in Jesus, and, "that the blood of Jesus Christ, his Son, cleanseth from all sin."

Those who came to Christ for healing, did not need, as

a condition of believing in Him, to understand the manner in which he would effect their cure. That, they probably never knew. They only needed to know that he was able and willing to do this thing for them. This they believed, and the work was wrought.

I have found this scriptural and old Wesleyan doctrine both safe and successful; and have no inclination to run after modern speculation on this subject. If adhered to, we will be saved from much unnecessary hairsplitting and division among themselves.

38
"Holiness to the Lord"

The history of the Church of God may be searched in vain, to find a parallel in attention to the great subject of personal holiness, such as has stirred the heart of Zion during the past forty years. "Holiness to the Lord," has become as never before, the great "central idea," in the tented grove, in the prayer service, in sacred song and religious testimony.

Tens of thousands hungering and thirsting after righteousness, have been refreshed and quickened, while great numbers have believed and entered into rest from inbred sin. This has been more or less the case in all sections of Protestant Christendom.

The obvious fact is, our people everywhere are feeling the need of a deeper, higher and more intensified spiritual life, and sympathize with every wholesome effort to secure it. The great felt want of the Christian church in our day is purity, and evangelical power, which in the divine economy are joined and inseparable.

During a few years past there has been a peaceful and happy disposition, generally prevalent in both ministry and laity, to dispense with needless speculation and controversy and seek by consecration, prayer and faith the cleansing blood of Jesus. How blessed is this! How glorious the victories achieved! How precious the baptisms of love received! And how many in all our churches are now walking in the clear light and on the high grounds of established holiness! How precious and delightful the Christian life! And how little of discord! Let God be praised and let his people rejoice!

A revival of personal holiness will secure and promote everything desirable in the love and unity, efficiency and aggressive power of the Church. Holiness becometh Zion—is her beauty and glory. It has in itself intrinsic excellence and power. Purity —sweet, moral Gospel purity—a whole constellation of virtues—perfect love, excluding hatred—perfect faith, excluding unbelief—perfect humility, excluding pride —perfect meekness, excluding anger, and perfect patience, excluding impatience.

Let God be praised! Here are riches and honors like the source whence they emanate—glorious as heaven and lasting as eternity. This holiness God enjoins and expects, and is himself the infinite model and source; and to secure this in every believer is the grand aim and object of the Gospel. For this purpose Christ died, the Holy Ghost is given, the means of grace instituted, and the Scriptures furnished.

"Holiness to the Lord" —how rich, glorious, and promising this aspect of Zion! This will make her life more intensified, her spiritual vision more clear, her spirit more joyful and happy, and make her safe and useful. It will save her from fearful relapses and backslidings, and send her on in her mighty mission in evangelizing this world for God.

How strange, that some Methodists do not appear to favor this work! Perhaps few openly oppose it, but how many practically reject it when it is clearly and specifically presented, and urged home as a present duty and privilege! Strange as it may appear, there is much of this in our own loved Church. While God is blessing thousands of precious souls through the land, Satan is not idle; and the old Moravian heresy is being taught again. There is great need of prayer and deep humiliation before God. How many, even among Methodists, treat this subject only in vague, ambiguous, indefinite generalities. How inconsistent to hold this precious doctrine in our theological propositions, and yet refuse to recognize it in our interior religious life!

Is not every Methodist preacher a son of that great and good man who said: "Therefore, let all our preachers preach Christian perfection *explicitly, clearly, constantly*, and let all our people see to it that they agonize for it?" The history of Methodism is a diary of Christian holiness, cutting its way through the icy walls of a nominal Christianity; and he who would rob it of its clear and specific teachings on this subject is an unworthy successor of the Wesleys.

39
SANCTIFICATION THROUGH THE TRUTH

CHRISTIAN SANCTIFICATION IS THROUGH, or, by the truth. "Sanctify them," (said Christ), "through thy truth. Thy word is truth." "The truth," is the Word of God, which is truth itself, and is divine, eternal, and infallible. Christ, who declared Himself "the Truth," is the essential, almighty "Word." The gospel is the "word of truth," and is the grand instrument, in the hand of the Holy Ghost, of Christian sanctification. This "word of truth," becomes to every believing soul a sanctifying emanation from the Holy Spirit, and is the vehicle of divine power to a lost world.

Religious truth is spiritual substance in religious things. "My truth," the truth of God, consists of the things of God *as they are*. Saving faith receives and appropriates these truths as they are, according to the revelation which God has made, and the soul is purified through their belief by the Spirit. Those truths are saving in their reception under the ministration of the Spirit, which, in the order of God, and the nature of things, stand related to personal salvation.

God's word is the authorized directory to the obtainment of this gracious state. As such it declares its necessity. How clear. "Follow after peace with all men, and the sanctification without which no man shall see the Lord." Heb. 12:12, R.V. "For this is the will of God, even your sanctification," I Thess. 4:3.

"The truth" directs to the efficient Agent in the work of purification, the Holy Spirit. "God hath from the beginning chosen you to salvation, through sanctification of the Spirit, and belief of the truth," 2 Thess. 2:13. "Seeing ye have purified your souls in obeying the truth, through the Spirit," I Peter 1:22.

The word of truth points out the meritorious and procuring cause of sanctification, the atoning and efficacious blood of Christ. His vicarious sacrifice as a sin offering is the central sanctifying truth of the gospel. "Who gave Himself for us, that He might redeem us from all iniquity and purify unto Himself, a peculiar people, zealous of good works." Titus 2:14. "The blood of Jesus Christ His Son cleanseth us from all sin," I John 1:7.

God's word of truth presents all needful hopes and motives, principles and inducements, to a life of holiness. "I beseech you therefore, brethren, by the mercies of God, that ye present your bodies a living sacrifice, holy, acceptable unto God, which is your reasonable service," Rom. 12:1. "Seeing that these things are thus all to be dissolved, what manner of persons ought ye to be in all holy living and godliness, looking for and earnestly desiring the coming of the day of God," 2 Peter 3:11, R.V. Here we are taught that the amazing scenes of the final dissolution of earthly things should exert a deep and abiding influence on us, and prompt to a holy and sanctified life.

The truth also gives us the receiving medium and immediate condition of sanctification; "Purifying their hearts by faith." The truth of God, received by faith, is brought into such vital contact with the heart, as to "purge it from dead (sinful) works to serve the living God." It is thus, we are sanctified "by the belief of the truth." To "believe on the Lord Jesus Christ," is to believe the truth, and every evangelical truth, being a beam of the "sun of righteousness," is saving in its nature. When the believing soul receives any saving truth, then grace begins to "reign through righteousness unto eternal life by Jesus Christ." Christ in His incarnation, earthly life and death, was the embodiment of all saving truth, and to entirely sanctify the soul, body and spirit of man, is the glorious objective point of the whole gospel system, inclusive of Christ's mission to our world.

All entirely sanctified souls know experimentally these blessed truths. They see that God in Christ, is revealed love; boundless, redeeming, pardoning, sanctifying and comforting love. They are "sanctified by the truth," and "rejoice in the truth." They are baptized "with the Spirit of faith," and triumph in Christ, "the living truth."

The Bible system of human salvation makes ample provision for the removal of all sin and pollution, and makes no allowance for any sin. Gospel salvation is salvation *from sin*, and never salvation *in sin*. Nothing can answer as a substitute for personal sanctification; no measure of benevolence, no fasting, no Christian works nor ordinances can answer as a substitute. These are valuable only as means of grace, to lead us to Christ, the truth, for personal purification.

Sanctification constitutes the only preparation for paradise. This preparation is to be accomplished *here, in this world, now, not in death, not in the grave, not at the resurrection, not in heaven.* Sanctification is to be wrought in the church militant, some time between regeneration and death. A complete deliverance from inbred sin must take place before we go hence.

To make us holy is the great design of Christianity. For

this the Son of God bled and died. For this He ever lives to make intercession for us. For this the Holy Spirit is given, and to cleanse and save us from sin is the main object of His gracious work.

40
CHARITY AND HUMILITY

MUCH HAS BEEN WRITTEN and said during the past forty years upon the subject of Entire Sanctification, more than ever before in the same length of time, in the history of the Church. This has been beneficial in calling general attention to the subject, and arousing the Church to the importance of a more thoroughly intensified spiritual life.

Many Christians, in all branches of the church, have been led to seek a better religious experience, and have taken advanced ground in both *theory* and *practice* on the subject of Christian holiness. The conviction has become more general in all. Christian lands, that the children of God should be holy, and possess the distinctive traits of Christian character, and the graces of the Spirit in their fullest perfection. Good men everywhere, are seeing more clearly, that for the accomplishment of her great work, the church must have a deeper experience, a greater enduement of power and a more complete conformity to the divine will.

While this pressing need is clearly seen and deeply

felt, yet there appears a growing inclination on the part of some to complain of those who either seek the experience and make profession of its attainment, or recommend others to give the subject special attention. These are often represented as "full of self-complacency," "self-confidence," and "possessed of a dogmatic and censorious spirit."

No doubt, in *manner, spirit* and *matter*, much of human imperfection has mingled with all that has been written or said regarding Christian sanctification. This is true of all subjects commanding human thought and activity. Nor is it denied, that some occasions have been given for the complaints heard, though they are often more imaginary than real, and not infrequently have no foundation in fact.

We by no means claim, that all the efforts of the friends of holiness are exempt from human frailties; indeed, we are painfully sensible that it is otherwise; but, that the complaints so often made, are facts to the extent represented, we do not believe, as many of those we see in print, we know to be without foundation.

The spirit, we hear, often attributed to the special advocates of full redemption, we do not *approve*, we do not *encourage*, and if seen we *deplore* and *denounce*. After more than a score of years with a very extended range of observation, we must say, we have not heard the many foolish, the many unwise and bitter things so frequently attributed to those teaching Entire Sanctification. Those devoted to this work are not blind to their danger, nor are they living without much watchfulness and prayer. They claim no perfection of manner, and are open to conviction of wrong of any kind, or of improprieties in any respect. Like all honest and earnest Christians, they can say, "Let the righteous smite me; it shall be a kindness; let him reprove me; it shall be an excellent oil, which shall not break my head."

Even in rebuking censoriousness, dogmatism, and self-confidence in others, we should carefully guard against being ourselves censorious, dogmatic, or self-confident.

It must be admitted, that there are very many formal, worldly, inactive and backslidden members in the church, and many plain things have been said and written (and very justly so), and no doubt, such as have assumed themselves assailed, have been under great temptation to impute a "spirit of pride," "self-complacency," or censoriousness," to those whom they have deemed their assailants, even though there may have been no grounds for such opinions.

It may be remembered, that no man ever pressed the church to be less worldly and more godly, without provoking the censure of some in the church. History, sacred or profane, furnishes no such examples. Christ, our blessed Lord, was constantly misrepresented and vilified. The apostles were called "babblers," and "fools," and represented as "mad," "drunk," and "beside themselves." The Scribes and Pharisees, thought St. Paul "self-righteous" when he declared to them, "I have lived in all good conscience before God." When they read from his pen, proclaiming to the world, "I can do all things through Christ which strengtheneth me," they doubtless thought him puffed up with self-conceit, and "in the very snare of the devil." Martin Luther, John Wesley, John Fletcher and Jonathan Edwards, did not escape the most severe imputations.

In the nature of things, any Christian who does his whole duty to the church and the world in their present state. speaking to them, and of them, as they really are, will incur the charge of censoriousness. Entire Sanctification implies the doing all our duty. In doing it, the facts respecting the church, the world, and the truth are to be treated with sincerity, honesty, and faithfulness; and this, in many cases, cannot be done without giving offense and incurring the charge of censoriousness. To maintain the contrary would impeach the wisdom and holiness of Jesus Christ himself.

So important and definite are the provisions for spiritual cleansing, and so precious the blessing, it is very easy and natural to speak and write strongly and earnestly with regard to it, and we may possibly at times expose ourselves to the imputations in question. Christian ministers have always been exposed to such charges, and those the most faithful and useful the most so. The truth uttered so as to be efficient, must be uttered in a manner indicating *importance, certainty* and *assurance*.

All good men have been painfully impressed with the difficulty of rebuking wickedness, and exposing fallacious and injurious sentiments in such a way as to avoid "*all appearance of evil.*"

41
REASONS WHY MORE ARE NOT ENTIRELY SANCTIFIED

ONE REASON IS, PEOPLE are not willing to *cleanse themselves*. Here is a part of the *purification*, in entire sanctification which every one must perform for himself. All "filthiness of the flesh" belongs to this class. God never does for any one what he can and ought to do himself.

The Lord requires not only holiness of heart, but purity of the body as well; and these in Christian sanctification must be united, and always are when the work is genuine. There is much *physical* depravity as well as moral depravity among partially purified saints. Entire sanctification includes a *radical* and *universal* purification of the entire man—soul and body. Hence, the body as well as the soul must be sanctified, and be kept clean and pure for God's service.

We are not to forget, that *chastity* of body is an important part of our sanctification. Sin is "filthiness," it may be of the *flesh*, or of the *spirit*, as there are defilements of the body and of the mind. There are sins of the "*flesh*" of which the body is the instrument, or that are committed by the body; and sins of the spirit, which are confined to the heart, and never develop in the outer life. We may and must be cleansed from both as God is to be glorified with both body and soul.

Doubtless many refuse to seek Christian holiness, because of habits of uncleanness, "filthiness of the flesh," or physical indulgences, which they are unwilling to give up or put away. No man can be entirely sanctified while his body is an "instrument of unrighteousness," in any sense, whether public or private.

God requires a pure soul in a chaste body. He made our bodies; they have been purchased for Him by the death of Christ, and they are not our own. "Ye are not your own, ye are bought with a price." The Christian's body is the temple of the Holy Ghost, and it is not to be profaned by prostitution to wicked uses, or filthy lusts. "If any man defile the temple of God, him shall God destroy."

Having made both body and soul, and redeemed both, He requires them empty as vessels fitted (purified) for His use. "Therefore glorify God in your body, and in your spirit, which are God's."

Many fail of entire sanctification, because they do not come out from among the ungodly, nor separate themselves from sinners. They are constantly *touching, tasting* or *handling* something that is unclean. Multitudes cannot be right with God, because they are wrong with men. There is much to be done in relation to our fellowmen, which we ourselves alone can do. This includes *honesty, honor, uprightness*, and all natural and moral virtues, as well as freedom from all unhallowed alliances with wicked men. There can be no purity, or spiritual life apart from outward morality.

Convictions, resolutions and good desires are not enough; there must be actual abandonment of all iniquity, and positive trusting the atonement of Christ that alone can sanctify the soul.

In repentance we turn from a life of sin, and put away all that can outwardly defile us; in regeneration the power of sinful habit is broken, and the new life, with the principle of holiness is implanted. The regenerate, in the light of the Holy Spirit and God's word, discovers in himself a remaining sinful nature, that pride, impatience, selfishness, and the love of the world are still within him, and hence, the need of a further cleansing in order to his purity—that he may be *"without spot, or wrinkle, or any such thing."* In entire sanctification the blood of Jesus Christ cleanseth the soul from all inbred sin, so that the whole nature, "spirit, soul and body," is pervaded with the Spirit of holiness.

42
NEEDLESS SINGULARITIES

CHRISTIAN SANCTIFICATION, THOUGH NOT identical with culture, social refinement and mere outside appearance, tends to promote every phase of manly, commendable excellence. Other circumstances being equal it will improve any man, every way and all ways.

It is to be regretted that some who claim to possess this purifying, ennobling grace are very careless in extravagant singularities, and in that way detract much from their usefulness. All who enjoy or claim to possess Christian purity should studiously avoid all things, little and great, that destroy the confidence of thoughtful people in them. Needless singularity is no mark of eminent holiness.

We ought to be all things to all men, in all matters where no questions of conscience are involved. In things perfectly indifferent we should conform to the customs and notions of those around us. This should be done just so far as we can do it with a good conscience and no further. St. Paul did this "for the gospel sake," "that he might by all means save some."

(See I Cor. 8:10-26.) We are not to yield at all to the customs or influences of others where personal duties and questions of enlightened conscience are concerned. In such instances, with meekness and humility, we are to be inflexible and as unbending as Cæsar's reed.

When our duty, our conscience and the plain Word of God require it, then we must be unyielding no matter how singular or different it may make us from others. There is a sense, as Mr. Wesley says, in which "we must be singular or be damned." Every holy life will appear singular to wicked men. "There are several acts of holiness," says Rev. William Burkitt, "which the profane world would esteem as madness, such as eminent self-denial, great seriousness in religion, their burning zeal, their holy singularity, their fervor of devotion, their patience and meekness under sufferings and reproaches." This blind and wicked world has always accounted religion as madness and frenzy. Even the apostles were said to be "mad," "drunk," and "beside themselves" they were called "babblers," "fools" and "fanatics."

While profound devotion to God will make us singular, different from others and separate from the world, it is to be feared some have made themselves odd, erratic and needlessly singular, for the sake of being singular and appearing eminently holy. This is a blunder that ought to be avoided. If Satan fails to keep us from coming out from the world, and of being separate from the world, he seeks to lead us clear over the line into needless singularity and extravagances. In this way he excites ridicule and contempt against real godliness. There should be no just grounds for this, and we should be wise as well as "pure in heart."

When we are needlessly singular in things purely indifferent, and are careless, slovenly and disgusting in crude oddities, in sensible people we create aversion and hatred against the doctrine and experience we would promote. Let all the professors of holiness, evince gravity, simplicity, modesty and decency. Let us pray for godly wisdom to avoid unnecessary awkwardness, slovenliness, sectarian cant, extreme mannerisms and profusion of witticisms. These are no manifestations or evidences of either justification or sanctification.

Let us study the Bible that our judgments may be enlightened, that we may "abstain from all appearance of evil." The Bible! the blessed Bible! is to be our instructor. It will teach us the true, the wise and the right way. The Bible and the Holy Spirit will guide us into all needful truth. Let us be Biblical in spirit and life, and avoid all foolish, outlandish mannerisms, and not give occasion for the good that is in us to be evil spoken of. God hath said, "If any of you lack wisdom, let him ask of God, and it shall be given him." Let us ask for it.

43
"SINLESS PERFECTION"

IT IS OFTEN ASSERTED that those who hold the doctrine and experience of entire sanctification believe in "sinless perfection" and teach its attainableness. This misrepresentation has been asserted over and over again, and by those who ought to know better. Those who reject the doctrine of Christian perfection will have it that we mean by it absolute or sinless perfection. Many who at times teach substantially just what we hold will oppose us, assuming that we believe in absolute perfection.

In a most excellent sermon by Dr. R. S. MacArthur, of the Calvary Baptist Church, New York, we have the following: "Do I here advocate doctrines of sinless perfection? If I did the verse following the text would rebuke me and contradict my teaching. In that verse it is distinctly said, 'If we say that we have not sinned, we make God a liar, and his word is not in us.' No man may claim sinless perfection. Such a claim as this the Apostle Paul never made, but distinctly repudiated."

While we repudiate the term sinless perfection in entire sanctification, we fail to see how Dr. MacArthur's proof-text meets the case. "If we say that we have not sinned," etc., in I John 1:10, has reference to sinning before God "forgives our sins, and cleanses us from all unrighteousness," and not after our pardon and purification. If he teaches that pardoned and purified Christians live in sin, and are sinning in any proper sense of those terms and in that view discards sinless perfection, we disclaim any such sentiment on that account.

If by sinless perfection be meant infallibility, or a state in which the soul cannot sin, we know of no one who holds any such nonsense, although it has been asserted over and over a thousand times by those opposed to Christian perfection.

If sinless perfection is understood to mean a perfect fulfillment of the Paradisiacal law of innocence and freedom from all involuntary transgressions of the law of love, we teach no such perfection. Mr. Wesley says, "Therefore, sinless perfection is a phrase I never use, lest I should seem to contradict myself. I believe a person filled with the love of God is still liable to these involuntary transgressions you may call sins, if you please; I do not." ("Plain Account," p. 67.)

On the contrary, if by this objectionable phrase be understood a perfect observance of the evangelical law of love, so as to love God with all the heart, soul and strength, this we believe the duty and privilege of every child of God. (See Deut. 30:6.)

If those who object to this term mean by it a gracious, moral condition in which the soul has no disposition to sin and will not sin, and by the grace of God is kept from sinning, in this sense we cannot object to it.

We give the following from Dr. MacArthur's sermon, which is just as all true Methodists teach: "Forgiveness were an indescribable blessing, but cleansing introduces us into a nobler condition and a sweeter relation. To forgive is to justify, but to cleanse is to sanctify as well as justify... For purification as well as pardon we must constantly strive. Careful study of the text (I John 1:9) shows us that it is a personal cleansing. The promise is that He will cleanse us from all unrighteousness... There must be a personal cleansing in the fountain opened for sin and cleansing. To that fountain I now invite you. Oh! come, wash and be clean now; yea, wash and be whiter than snow!... There is only one fountain that can wash away the stain of sin. Oh, come to that fountain now, wash and be clean. We observe also that it is a perfect cleansing— 'cleanse us from all unrighteousness.' The sin which abides in the heart as conscious guilt may be removed by God's pardon. The sin which abides in us as pollution requires divine cleansing... It is the duty and privilege of every child of God to have his heart cleansed from remaining depravity, and to keep himself unspotted from the world." Here we have from this eminent Baptist divine the doctrine of entire sanctification just as it is held by the advocates of Christian sanctification in the Methodist Church and in all the holiness associations. But we believe not only in teaching it, but in obtaining it, living in it and glorifying God in its possession.

44
MISTAKES REGARDING ENTIRE SANCTIFICATION

A VERY COMMON MISTAKE among many professing Christians is in overrating Christian sanctification. While some underrate it many more overrate it; they can hardly think of a perfect Christian or a holy man as anything less than an angelic being in human shape. They do not seem to think that the words "perfection," "holiness" and "sanctification" used in this connection are modified by the term Christian. It is Christian holiness, Christian perfection and Christian sanctification. It is not angelic nor Adamic.

All the works of God are perfect in their order and various kinds. There is a gradation which belongs to all the works of God, and hence there are various kinds and degrees of perfection. Each sphere of being has its normal limits; God alone has absolute, infinite perfection; angels are perfect in their order and sphere, but they fall infinitely below the perfection of God. Man has his sphere, and though fallen, in the mediatorial economy his present highest, practicable rectitude is his perfection—and is Christian perfection.

A Christian who is wholly sanctified is perfect as a Christian, not perfect as an angel, nor as perfect as he will be when he goes where the angels are. Christ declares that he will then be "equal unto the angels." Here in this life we are to be "perfect in love," in grace and the graces of a Christian.

In this life all who are entirely sanctified are possessed of a frail body and infirmities of mind. Our bodies and souls are closely united, and whatever affects the one affects the other. Whatever the moral condition of our souls, the frailty of our bodies often weakens our animation of mind, depresses our spirits, taxes our patience and produces heaviness though the heart retains its purity and integrity.

The infirmities of the mind are many in this life even in the holiest of men. There is weakness of understanding, slowness of apprehension, frailty of memory, irregular imagination and imperfect judgment. These affect all men, good or bad, more or less in our present state of being. These cause many imperfections in conduct which are not sins, and do not necessarily affect the holiness of the heart. The purest and wisest of men are subjects of much ignorance, as it is not given to any man to know everything, and consequently all are liable to errors and mistakes, and these lead to errors in life and practice in things which have no moral quality, and hence are not sinful or transgressions of the law of love. As a sample, a holy man may be sick and take a medicine which he hopes will cure him, but it hastens him out of the world. Another is misinformed concerning the character of a person, and consequently treats him with more or less confidence than is wise and proper. A thousand similar mistakes may occur in those cleansed from all sin, and in possession of pure love to God and their neighbor.

45
ENTIRE SANCTIFICATION DISTINCT FROM JUSTIFICATION AND REGENERATION

JUSTIFICATION AND REGENERATION precede and lay the foundation for entire sanctification, and there is a transition from regeneration to complete purification.

Justification and the forgiveness of sins are synonymous. Each express an act of mercy in the mind of God, that blots out our actual transgressions and absolves us from all guilt. All such can say: "There is therefore now no condemnation to them which are in Christ Jesus," and "Being justified (pardoned) by faith we have peace with God."

"Regeneration," "Born again," "Born of the Spirit," "Born from above," signify the renewal of our nature and the impartation of spiritual life, a work wrought in the soul, which accompanies justification, and is one of the evidences of it.

"Sanctification," "wholly sanctified," "perfection," "perfect holiness," "perfect love," imply a personal cleansing or moral condition as distinctly known, and identified with as much certainty as justification and regeneration. It has its marks and signs and evidences as a distinct work.

There is as clear and distinct conviction in the regenerate preceding entire sanctification, as that which preceded justification or pardon in the penitent sinner. In the one case it is conviction of guilt and need of pardon, and in the other it is conviction of "inbred sin," and need of purity.

Soon after regeneration, the conviction is felt, though converted and forgiven, that there still remains in the heart "indwelling sin," real, living, stirring bosom evils, which need extermination. After conversion the mind is enlightened to see more clearly its own natural depravity, moral condition and deficiency. The extent and purity of God's law is seen more clearly, and the necessity of a purified heart to obey its precepts and love God with all the heart.

After conversion the conscience becomes more tender and active, and the cravings of the soul for communion and fellowship with God become more intense. In this condition there is a conviction of moral deficiency, and the need of entire sanctification, and a desire for it, which is a spontaneity in the regenerate heart.

Sometimes, the distress and struggles of the Christian believer seeking purity, or deliverance from indwelling sin, are more severe than those in seeking pardoning mercy. This is frequently the case with those who were converted in early life, and never had those painful and overwhelming convictions which some have.

Some believers are convicted for years of their need of full cleansing before they receive it, while others very soon after their conversion seek and obtain clean hearts. Some grieve the Holy Spirit by refusing to yield to His influences and they become cold, formal and gradually backslide from God. The Holy Spirit and the Bible show them their great privilege and duty, and through unbelief, or prejudice, or Satanic influences, they refuse to follow their light, and like ancient Israel, while in sight of the promised land, give way to unbelief, and wander in the wilderness for years to come.

Others see their privilege and duty, and admit it, but are not willing to fully submit to God, or give up their bosom sins. They keep back part of the price, like poor Ananias and Sapphira, and if they are not struck dead at once, they become lukewarm and spiritually dead, and unless they repent and return to God, will utterly apostatize. This is the class in our churches who are full of doubts, sore conflicts, trials, severe temptations and dissatisfaction.

On the contrary, those who walk in the light, yield fully to God, and trust in the promise and blood of Jesus, experience a radical purification from all moral corruption, and enjoy "the fullness of the blessing of Christ." The evidences of their purification are as clear and assuring as those of their justification, with its attendant blessings. Purity of heart is as strongly and clearly marked, as the regeneration of the heart, and is as divinely attested by the witness of the Spirit.

46
THE HOLINESS AND HAPPINESS OF ALL MEN

I DESIRE TO PRESENT some thoughts on the question of the holiness and happiness of all men. I make no claim to special originality, but aim to present the truth gathered from any source available, without regard to quotation marks or names, which would add nothing to their strength of logic, truth or argument. The inspired direction is: "Let no man deceive you with vain words: for because of these things cometh the wrath of God upon the children of disobedience." —Eph. 5:6.

Are all men to be finally holy and happy? This is the most momentous question which ever engaged the attention of man. It involves interests as high as heaven and as lasting as immortality. The settlement of this question is connected with the dearest interests of our spirits while the throne of God shall stand or angels sing.

In this question each and all have a common interest. Such is the magnitude of the interests involved; in discussing the subject there should be the utmost candor and thoroughness. Lightness in the treatment of such a subject is seriously out of place. The flippant and careless manner in which some treat it commends itself to no reverent or candid mind.

I desire to consider the most common and plausible arguments presented in favor of the salvation of all men, and against the future and endless punishment of the finally impenitent.

It is argued and claimed by some that all men will finally be holy and happy, drawn from the perfections of God. All will admit that all the divine perfections are infinite and in view of our incapacity to comprehend infinity, it cannot be claimed that God can make a full revelation of his perfections to us. The moral and natural attributes of God can be fully known only by himself. If this be so any conclusions drawn from the divine perfections, are drawn from premises which we do not fully understand. Such conclusions, in the nature of the case, must be as uncertain as our knowledge of the premises is imperfect A false method necessarily leads to a false conclusion.

In this way men often reason as follows: God is infinitely good and God is infinitely powerful. As he is infinitely good, he would not create his creatures subject to any evil whatever; and as he is infinitely powerful, he can accomplish all his purposes; therefore all his creatures are free from all evil and perfectly happy. This method of reasoning leads to conclusions contradicted by nature and revelation.

We can determine what is and what is not consistent with the perfections of God only by what we know and see to actually exist, or from what God has revealed in the Scriptures. If it can be proved from facts as they actually exist, or from the Bible, that all men will be saved, then we must admit that it is consistent with the divine perfections to save all men, including all those who reject Christ, and die in sin and rejection of his authority.

On the other hand, if present facts indicate and the Bible positively teaches, that some men, through their sins and rejection of Christ, will be "punished with everlasting destruction from the presence of the Lord and from the glory of his power, it must be admitted that eternal punishment may be consistent with the divine attributes, though we may not be able to see the reason in those perfections why it should be so. We see many things and facts in the providence of God for which we can see no reason in the divine attributes.

If the perfections of God would enable us to determine just the demerit and desert of sin, then it might be made to appear that "eternal damnation" is inconsistent with divine justice and goodness. Who, but God can determine the turpitude, criminality and the extent of the evil of sin, and what and how much punishment the sinner is liable to endure? As God views it he asks, "How can ye escape the damnation of hell?"

No man can prove from the perfection of God, independently of revelation, either the immortality of the soul, the resurrection of the body or a future state; how, then, can he prove from them the final salvation of all men? The perfections of God, if they prove anything on this subject, prove the doctrine of future retribution. We know that whatever does exist, must exist consistent with the divine perfections. We cannot prove from those perfections that the existence of sin and misery is consistent with such perfections, yet this can be proved from fact; for sin and misery do exist, and therefore we know from their actual existence that they can exist consistently with the perfections of God.

Facts bear only on one side of this question, hence, matter of fact cannot prove that it is consistent with the perfections of God to save all men, whatever may be their conduct, for all men are not now saved. Sin and misery have existed for six thousand years and now exist, and hence their existence must be consistent with the divine attributes, and as those attributes are unchangeable, the inference is a fair one that it may always be consistent with the divine perfections that sin and misery should exist.

It is claimed that all men will be finally holy and happy because "God is love" and infinitely benevolent, and that his love is underived and eternal. We admit the infinite love of God and also that it is underived and eternal; but deny that it follows from thence that all men will become holy and happy. God's infinite love has always existed, and as it did not originally prevent sin and misery, but has permitted it for thousands of years past, how can it be shown that his love will save those of whom Christ declares, "They shall be forgiven neither in this world, neither in the world to come?"

As God's infinite love and wisdom did not keep man holy and happy when he was so, how can it be shown the final holiness and happiness of all men will be secured by his love and wisdom? The argument drawn from the love and wisdom of God would have applied to Adam and Eve in Eden, in proof that they could never become unholy and unhappy with the same propriety that it does to us in proof that we cannot remain unholy and unhappy. All can see that this argument will apply backward to the condition of men for six thousand years past, as well as forward to his condition for six thousand or more years to come. As the argument is false as to what is past and present, how can it be relied upon to prove what is to come?

For God to be love is one thing, and for intelligent, voluntary accountable beings to insult and reject that love is another thing. St. Paul says, "If any man love not the Lord Jesus Christ, let him be accursed." God loves all men as his creatures; but all men do not love God as their Creator. God loves sinners now, but sinners do not love God, and no man can be holy and happy who does not love God. The objector should prove that all men will love God endlessly, and not assume that because God's love is endless, all men on that account will be holy and happy. If present infinite love and wisdom do not secure the present holiness and happiness of the sinner, it is assuming too much that endless love and wisdom will produce endless holiness and happiness.

It is claimed that all men will finally become holy and happy because of the almighty power of God. That God is almighty, no one disputes, but what God can do when his power alone is consulted, and what he can consistently do in view of all the perfections of his nature and the nature and relation of responsible moral intelligences, are quite different from each other. Power is ability to perform. God has power to do anything that is an object of physical force, or anything which, in the nature of things, can be done. His almighty power is guided by his infinite wisdom, and it never breaks over the sacred bounds of eternal truth. It is no limitation of divine omnipotence to say it cannot work contradictions. To say that God can work contradictions would not magnify his power, but expose our own absurdity. Omnipotence cannot cause a thing to be, or not to be, at the same time; or make two and two equal five. Such things are absurdities, and not the objects of power.

Omnipotence cannot necessitate virtue. A necessitated virtue would be a contradiction and an absurdity. Nothing can be virtue which is produced by extraneous physical force. Universal reason and consciousness affirm this. A necessitated volition is a contradiction in terms. It is absurd to suppose that moral and accountable agents can be governed and made virtuous in another way than by moral means. It is not more absurd to suppose that God could swing the worlds through space by moral power than to suppose that he governs the moral universe by physical power.

Physical power, guided by infinite wisdom and goodness, has created moral beings and endowed them with the most exalted attributes and moral powers; but the virtue or holiness of such responsible beings does not consist in the possession of such moral powers, but in the right and obedient exercise of those powers.

A necessitated virtue being an absurdity, a contradiction in terms, it is clear that sin and woe may enter into the best moral world, and the divine perfections are consistent with their existence. We are willing to admit that God might have avoided sin by putting man lower in the scale of being; by filling the world with uncounted millions of idiots, or with creatures even lower down than idiots; but he has not seen wise to do it. If virtue and happiness could be necessitated in all moral, voluntary intelligences, no doubt but God would cause them to shine out in all parts of his dominion, and not a blot of sin would be seen upon the beauty of the world.

God's abhorrence of sin and his approbation of virtue are seen in the dispensations of natural good and evil, of pleasure and pain. The design of this divine arrangement is to prevent the commission of sin and secure the practice of virtue, which cannot be produced by the direct omnipotency of his power. There is a sense in which God sincerely desires the happiness of all men, just as he sincerely desires all men to obey him; but his desire for their happiness will not be secured, just as his desire that all men shall love him and obey him, and do his will now, is not secured; because it is impossible in the nature of things to necessitate voluntary obedience or holiness.

God does the best that infinite wisdom and goodness can do for the happiness and well-being of all his creatures; but voluntary agents have the power to obstinately work out their own ruin and destruction. Omnipotence cannot, in the nature of the case, confer holiness and happiness upon them (that being a question of voluntary agency and not of omnipotent power), and they do not choose to acquire it. All such are asked, "What more could I have done for my vineyard, that I have not done in it?"

It is not true that all men are always punished for their own good. A felon is not incarcerated, or a murderer put to death for his own benefit. State prisons are built for the good of community and the protection of the innocent, and not for the correction and well being of criminals. God did not drown the antediluvians, nor burn Sodom for their correction and benefit, but as he tells us: "Making them an example unto those that after should live ungodly." 2 Peter 2:4.

If punishment for a single year is justified on the ground that it is necessary to support government for a single year, is endless punishment in support of the eternal moral government of God, a greater anomaly than temporal punishments in relation to temporal governments? If temporal punishments are justified because they are necessary to meet the exigencies and uphold the interests of temporal governments, it cannot be shown that eternal punishments may not be justified in relation to an eternal government.

The idea that all punishment is corrective entirely overlooks the sinner's desert. What the sinner deserves as a just punishment for his sins and what he needs as a remedy for his spiritual disease, are two distinct points vastly different from each other. To suppose that all punishment is designed to make the sinner better, is to say that he deserves no punishment as a reward for his sins, but needs it as a remedy for his disease. This is both absurd and unscriptural. The Scriptures represent the sinner as guilty and deserving of punishment, and his punishment as a curse and not a blessing.

The Bible tells us: "Christ hath redeemed us from the

curse of the law" — Gal. 3:13. By the curse of the law, must be meant penalty or punishment. If all punishment is reformatory, then Christ redeemed us from what would have done us good. "Who hath warned you to flee from wrath to come?" Matt. 3:7. Matthew, here must mean punishment. "The law worketh wrath." Rom. 4:15. How can this be if punishment is a merciful remedy for our spiritual diseases? St. James says, "Sin when it is finished bringeth forth death." This popular argument says, when sin is finished it bringeth forth life. Which is right?

"Who shall be punished with everlasting destruction." 2 Thess. 1:9. What then is the everlasting destruction with which the sinner is threatened? According to this argument, it is the only gracious and efficient means which God can employ to make sinners good and happy.

If all punishment is corrective, then when punishment ceases to be corrective, it ceases to be just; and all incorrigible transgressors, who are made no better by punishment, are unjustly punished and should be released at once, because they are too inveterate to be reformed. This would throw all our prison doors open at once to a large share of their inmates.

The Scriptures represent the sinner as being punished according to his works and not according to his wants. Every man is represented as receiving "according to that he hath done in the body" and not to that which is necessary to save him. Christ says, "Behold I come quickly and my reward is with me to give to every man according as his works shall be," not according to what is necessary to bring him to repentance. The sinner is said to be cursed, to be punished, to endure "wrath," wrath without mixture," indignation, and to perish. If all these are only for the sinner's good, then are wrath and love the same; then between vengeance and mercy there is no difference, then an effect proves a remedy for its cause, then is a curse a blessing and death leads to life.

The dispensations of natural providence, as well as the express declarations of the Bible, forbid the inference that God desires the happiness of those who obstinately persist in sin. Their united language is, "Woe unto the wicked, it shall be ill with him." God desires the happiness of the obedient and virtuous; "Say ye to the righteous it shall be well with him."

The error of the argument drawn from the fatherhood of God, is in magnifying the paternal character of God, at the expense of His infinite holiness and justice, as the sovereign ruler and judge of the universe. While God, by creation and providence, is the father of all men, He is also law giver, ruler and judge of all men.

Any argument that destroys or obscures the immutable harmony and equality of the divine perfections, His justice, holiness and truth, as well as His goodness, wisdom and fatherhood must be dangerously false. In this argument the love and paternal character of God are so exalted as to render his other perfections and his relations to man subservient to these in order to reach the conclusion that all men will become holy and happy. By the same process of reasoning from the holiness, justice and truth of God (which are infinite), a directly opposite conclusion may be obtained.

For example: The infinite justice and holiness of God must prompt Him to inflict the greatest possible punishment upon all who violate His law and oppose His holiness. All sinners have insulted the infinite holiness of God, violated His holy law, and are amenable to His infinite justice. God's infinite holiness and justice cannot be impeached, therefore all incorrigible sinners must be eternally miserable. This argument from the justice and holiness of God for the "eternal damnation" of the wicked, is just as strong as that drawn from the goodness and love of God for the "eternal salvation" of all men.

Any mode of reasoning that will support conclusions

so diametrically opposite, is too weak to rest our hopes of heaven upon. It is not true that all men are the children of God in the paternal, religious sense that Christians are, who are "born of that spirit" and are the "sons of God." Adam was a son of God, in a sense his posterity are not. God was his immediate creator, both of body and soul, and he was created holy and possessed the moral image of God; but he sinned, forfeited the image of God, incurred His displeasure and became an outlaw and plunged his posterity into a state of moral degeneracy, in which they can become the children of God only by grace, adoption and salvation; see Rom. 8:15; John 8:47. Men, in their sinful state, are called in the scriptures, "Children of the world," "Children of disobedience," "Children of the wicked one," and "Children of the devil." We are expressly told, Rom. 9:8, "they which are the children of the flesh, these are not the children of God;" see Eph. 2:2, John 13:8 and John 3:10.

It has often been asked, after depicting and caricaturing the horrors of the lost, "Are you not better than your God? Would you punish one of your children endlessly?" This appeal to human sympathies is both deceptive and fallacious. It lies with all its weight against matter of fact, the present sufferings of the human race. God has seen and heard all the wails, agonies, tears and sorrows of six thousand years of human depravity and woe and He has almighty power, and yet he does not relieve matters. The world suffers on age after age and some think it is growing worse and worse. It is clearly seen that this popular argument, making blind human sympathy a rule by which to judge of God's moral government over wicked men, is most preposterous.

Another plausible argument, often given as proof of the final holiness and happiness of all men, is the corrective nature and design of punishment. The argument is usually as follows: "All divine punishment is designed to reform the sufferer; but endless punishment cannot reform the sufferer, therefore, no divine punishment can be endless." It is said, "The woes of sin are its antidote," and "if there be suffering in the next world, it is as in this, but the medicine of the sickly soul."

In this, truth is adroitly mixed with error. All good men believe that "suffering comes from wrong doing, and wellbeing from virtue; but it does not therefore follow that the woes of sin are its antidote either in this world or in the next. If God designs to reform sinners by the woes of sin, He certainly fails in His object, as millions of men sin and suffer the woes of sin all their lives and grow worse until they die. The position that "the woes of sin are its antidote," is the same as saying that an effect will change or cure its cause, which is a philosophical blunder.

The fallacy of this popular argument, is in the main position, which asserts that all punishment is designed to reform the sufferer. This position is not true. That God does sometimes correct with a view to the reformation of the subject, we readily admit; but such corrective dispensations are usually confined to them who are the people of God, in distinction from others, and are always limited to this life during which sinners are in a gracious state of probation.

Because God corrects His children to render them more holy and useful, or because He punishes sinners during their day of gracious probation, to bring them to repentance, to infer from this that all punishment, under all circumstances, is designed to reform the sufferer, is a conclusion much broader than the premises from which it is drawn. It is a fact which all can see that the discipline which is a "savor of life unto life" with some, is a "savor of death unto death" with others. This is a distinctly revealed doctrine of the New Testament. "God knows how to deliver the godly out of temptation, and to reserve the unjust unto the day of judgment to be punished."

While God desires all men to be holy and happy, some will not be because a compulsory holiness is impossible, some will not work out for themselves what cannot be wrought out for them, without their agency, even by Omnipotence. The divine expostulation to such is, "As I live, saith the Lord God, I have no pleasure in the death of the wicked; but that the wicked turn from his way and live, turn ye, turn ye from your evil ways, for why will ye die." Ezek. 33:11.

In view of this, our Savior declared, "Ye will not come unto me that ye might have life." God hates sin above all things. "Oh do not this abominable thing which I hate." Sin is the ruinous thing in the universe and God forbids it, and is anxious to prevent it, and he does all His infinite wisdom and power can to prevent it. It cannot be shown that the Almighty could have done more than He has actually done to prevent sin and secure holiness without doing violence to the nature of man as a moral accountable being.

Nor can be shown that the means and measures, both as to kind and degree, employed by God for the salvation and happiness of man from sin and misery, have not been precisely such as to secure the maximum of good and the minimum of evil. We vindicate the character and power of God in the existence of sin and misery in the world, on the ground that there is an inherent impossibility in excluding all evil from a moral universe. It is a moral impossibility for God to do wrong. God cannot lie and He has said, "The wicked shall be turned into hell and all the nations that forget God." If hell means the grave, we may add everybody else.

God has the same power to annihilate a limited punishment and hell, that He has to annihilate eternal punishment and hell; but this he does not see fit to do. Sin, sorrow and death have reigned in this world for nearly six thousand years. God has no more power to destroy sin and misery than He had to prevent them. If His power has slumbered over the horrible reign of sin and misery, over its sighs and groans and death during these long thousands of years, since He drove the guilty pair out of Paradise, no argument can be drawn from the power of God to prove that he will ever see it consistent to destroy sin and misery, or annihilate its wicked subjects. Of the finally impenitent He has said, "These shall go away into everlasting punishment."

Again it is said and argued that the holiness of God assures the final holiness and happiness of all men. It is said a holy God cannot perpetuate unholiness forever. This statement rests upon an assumed absurdity, i. e., if all men are not saved, a holy God perpetuates unholiness forever. If sin and misery cannot exist forever without being perpetuated by God, then they cannot exist for six thousand years without being perpetuated by Him for that time, and if a holy God can perpetuate sin and unholiness for six thousand years, His holiness cannot be incompatible with their eternal existence. The stupendous idea of eternity attaches to the whole of time as well as to a part, and so far as the holiness of God determines anything, it will determine it in respect to a part of eternity, as well as to the whole of it.

It is claimed that all men will finally become holy and happy, because of the Fatherhood of God. It is said God is the father of all men and that a good father, if he had the power, would not permit his children to suffer except for their good. God has the power and therefore will not permit suffering, except for the good of His offspring. This position is untrue in both of its parts. God does not act toward the family of man as a good, earthly parent would act toward his children, if he had the power, nor could he do so without a violation of the principles of truth and righteousness. A good earthly parent, if he had the power, would not allow his child to become a thief, or a drunkard, or a blasphemer, or murderer; but God, having the power to prevent it (as claimed by some), does permit every degree of crime. A good earthly parent would not allow his children to suffer excruciating pain by fire, accident or poison, yet God permits these. A good earthly parent, if he had the power to prevent it, would not allow one child to wrong, oppress or murder another, nor would he allow his children to become insane, or to blaspheme the name of their father, or to injure his interests, yet God allows all these things among the human family.

The providence of God, every day, is a practical refutation of this argument. He is now doing, and has been ever since the fall of man, what no earthly parent would do, or would be allowed to do by any civil government. What good father would drown his whole family as God drowned the antediluvian world?

What father would burn his children as God burned the five cities of the plain, sending fire from heaven, consuming men, women and children? What father would send serpents among his children, or open the ground and swallow them up, or kill them by the thousands by volcanoes and earthquakes? What father who could prevent it, would permit his children to starve and perish by millions, as God has allowed whole nations to perish by famine, plague and war?

If God can drown, burn and destroy His children with famine, earthquakes and pestilence and death for so many thousand years, and still be a good father, as is claimed, how strong is the argument drawn from his loving fatherhood, in proof that He will never do what He declares he will do, "sever the wicked from the just, and cast them into the furnace of fire; there shall be wailing and gnashing of teeth." Math. 13:47-50.

The sympathies and feelings of our nature are often

presented as a reason why all men will ultimately become holy and happy. If our short-sighted sympathies and feelings are a standard of truth, then we need neither reason nor revelation to help us to our creed in respect to the administration of the moral government of God. That our feelings and sympathies are shocked at the Bible statements regarding the condition of the finally impenitent, we admit, and we infer from it that they are designed to prompt us "to flee from wrath to come" and not to teach us that there is no "wrath to come." This looks consistent and natural. If we had nothing within us that would shudder at the idea of punishment, we would have no inducement to make our escape from it, and yet, because we shudder at the idea of endless punishment, some conclude that there can be no such thing. "Such pervert the right ways of the Lord."

The argument proves too much, it runs into absurdities and contradicts matter of fact. It would disprove the justice of any punishment at all, to say nothing of God's providence towards guilty offenders in all ages. Our feelings revolt at the idea of God burning the Sodomites for licentiousness, and striking dead Ananias and Sapphira for lying, and sending out fire from himself to consume two hundred and fifty men for offering him a mock service, and smiting with instant death the ten spies for unbelief, and punishing with a horrible death Achan and all his family for covetousness and doing the same with Korah, Dathan and Abiram, with their wives, sons and little children for rebellion, sending a plague to sweep away fourteen thousand of his people for murmuring against his servants, and directing Moses to slay three thousand men for dancing around a golden calf, and sending a destroying angel to kill twenty thousand Israelites for idolatry.

The filial relations and tender ties that bind humanity together are presented in proof that all men will finally become holy and happy. Appeals are often made to mothers and friends whether they could enjoy heaven, or would desire to go there if their loved ones are excluded? Some even go so far as to say they have no wish to go to heaven if their friends are not saved. This popular appeal is more plausible than reasonable.

It assumes as truth what experience denies; the very persons who make it contradict the principle it involves, by not refusing wealth, honor or happiness because all their friends are not wealthy, honored or happy. This argument pushed to its logical results would prove that good men cannot enjoy the rewards of virtue because the disobedient are punished for their vice; that liberty cannot be enjoyed because the lawless are confined in prisons; that life to the good can be no blessing because the felon is hung. Both experience and common sense refute such arguments to prove that all men will become holy and happy.

We have noticed the strongest and most plausible positions taken to prove the final happiness of all men. If our replies to them are irrelevant, or illogical and fallacious, we shall be glad to know it. To ridicule and caricature endless punishment proves nothing except the weakness and depravity of those who do it. Those who expect all will finally be saved, and base their hopes upon that, make their salvation to depend upon a disputed point; disputed not only by the principal writers and commentators of every age, but by the mass of the whole Christian world.

Those who neglect personal salvation and rely upon the ultimate salvation of all, hang their eternal salvation upon contested points, rejected by every evangelical church. If the churches are right and they are mistaken, their prospects are blasted in eternal night. All who live Christian lives are safe anyway; if there be no eternal hell, the believing there is one, cannot expose them to one. If there be no "eternal damnation" they cannot be eternally damned. "Their rock is not as our rock, our enemies themselves being judges."

Members of Schmul's Wesleyan Book Club buy these outstanding books at 40% off the retail price.

Join Schmul's Wesleyan Book Club by calling toll-free:
800-$S_7P_7B_2O_6O_6K_5S_7$
Put a discount Christian bookstore in your own mailbox.

Visit us on the Internet at
www.wesleyanbooks.com

You may also order direct from the publisher by writing:
Schmul Publishing Company
PO Box 776
Nicholasville, KY 40340

www.ingramcontent.com/pod-product-compliance
Lightning Source LLC
Chambersburg PA
CBHW070147100426
42743CB00013B/2842